THE KINGFISHER
YOUNG PEOPLE'S BOOK OF
OCEANS

THE KINGFISHER
YOUNG PEOPLE'S BOOK OF
OCEANS

DAVID LAMBERT

KING*f*ISHER

NEW YORK

Author: David Lambert
Consultant: Dr. Denise Smythe-Wright
Editor: Clive Wilson
U.S. Editor: Aimee Blythe
Designer: Jacqueline Palmer
Art Editor: Sue Aldworth
Cover Composite: Bernard Gudynas
Picture Researcher: Veneta Bullen
Researcher: Amanda Francis

KINGFISHER
Larousse Kingfisher Chambers Inc.
95 Madison Avenue
New York, New York 10016

First edition 1997
4 6 8 10 9 7 5 3
3(TR)/1099/TWP/NEW/150NYMA

LIBRARY OF CONGRESS CATALOGING-IN-PUBLICATION DATA
Lambert, David.
The Kingfisher young people's book of oceans / David Lambert.
—1st American ed.
p. cm.
Includes index.
Summary: Presents information about the world's oceans, how they
were formed, their geology, tides, waves, sea life, coasts,
resources provided by oceans, myths and legends about the oceans, and
more.
1. Ocean—Juvenile literature. [1. Ocean.] I. Kingfisher
Books. II. Title.
GC21.5.L329 1997
551.46—dc21 96-50971 CIP AC

ISBN: 0-7534-5098-4
Printed in Singapore

CONTENTS

Introduction

Oceans cover more than two-thirds of our planet's surface. A ship could sail around the world without touching land and, if it sank, would probably plunge more than 10,000 feet (3,000 m) before reaching the seabed.

These vast, hidden depths are home to millions of different plants and animals. Oceans also support life on dry land. All land plants and animals evolved in ancient seas. Even today, we could not survive without the oceans. They act like giant heaters, spreading the Sun's warmth around the globe. These vast reservoirs of water also recycle rain, preventing continents from turning to deserts. They supply us with seafood, and their colossal stores of oil, gas, and minerals help to fuel today's civilization.

Continents split the deep into four connected basins, containing the Pacific, Atlantic, Indian, and Arctic Oceans. The Pacific Ocean, the largest and deepest, could hold every continent, or the water of the other three oceans. The Arctic is the smallest, shallowest, and coldest ocean of all.

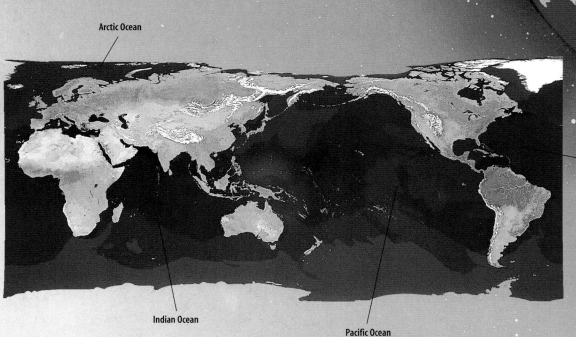

Arctic Ocean

Indian Ocean

Pacific Ocean

Atlantic Ocean

◁ There are four main oceans—the Pacific, the Atlantic, the Arctic, and the Indian. Together they cover more than two-thirds of the Earth's surface.

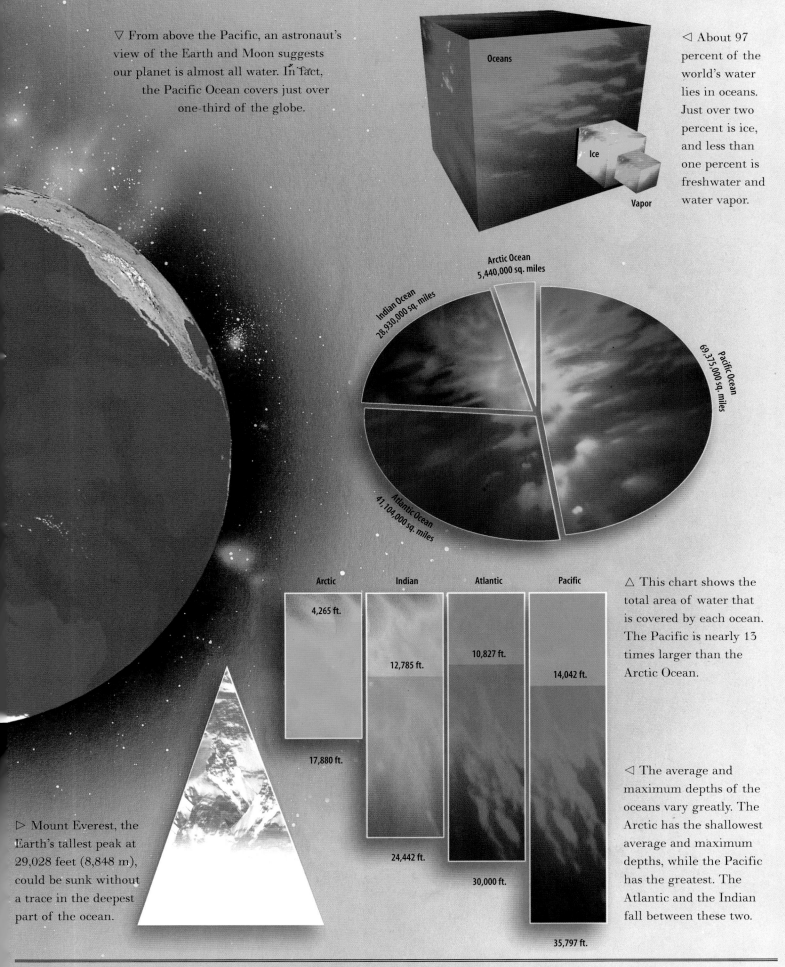

▽ From above the Pacific, an astronaut's view of the Earth and Moon suggests our planet is almost all water. In fact, the Pacific Ocean covers just over one-third of the globe.

Oceans

Ice

Vapor

◁ About 97 percent of the world's water lies in oceans. Just over two percent is ice, and less than one percent is freshwater and water vapor.

Arctic Ocean
5,440,000 sq. miles

Indian Ocean
28,930,000 sq. miles

Pacific Ocean
69,375,000 sq. miles

Atlantic Ocean
41,104,000 sq. miles

Arctic

4,265 ft.

17,880 ft.

Indian

12,785 ft.

24,442 ft.

Atlantic

10,827 ft.

30,000 ft.

Pacific

14,042 ft.

35,797 ft.

△ This chart shows the total area of water that is covered by each ocean. The Pacific is nearly 13 times larger than the Arctic Ocean.

▷ Mount Everest, the Earth's tallest peak at 29,028 feet (8,848 m), could be sunk without a trace in the deepest part of the ocean.

◁ The average and maximum depths of the oceans vary greatly. The Arctic has the shallowest average and maximum depths, while the Pacific has the greatest. The Atlantic and the Indian fall between these two.

Evolving Oceans

Parts of some facing coastlines look as though they once fit together. In 1915, the German scientist Alfred Wegener suggested a reason for this. He believed today's continents are the remains of a vast supercontinent that broke into fragments and drifted apart. Half a century later, scientists were discovering how this theory of "continental drift" worked. The Earth's outer layer consists of mobile plates of thick continental crust and thinner oceanic crust. Both float on a hot, dense layer of rock called the mantle. The Earth's inner heat stirs currents in the mantle, which help to remake the ocean floor, shuffle continents around, and push up mountains where plates collide. The continual spreading of the seafloor creates new oceanic crust and gets rid of the old material. None survives longer than 200 million years—a fraction of the age of continents. This process does not mean all oceans stay the same size. The Atlantic is growing, but the Pacific shrinks as the American continental plates override its eastern rim.

△ This pillow lava is new sea-floor spewed from a crack in a spreading ridge 6,135 feet (1,870 m) deep.

△ Two hundred million years ago there was one huge supercontinent (1). This had split up by 100 million years ago (2). Fifty million years ago the Atlantic was just opening up (3). In 50 million years' time the Earth will have changed again (4).

▽ A jigsaw of tectonic plates forms ocean floors and carries continents. These plates jostle around, sometimes colliding, sometimes moving away from each other. Most volcanoes and earthquakes happen where plates meet.

Upper mantle

→ Direction of plate movement

⌒ Divergent boundary

⌒ Convergent boundary

⋙ Transform fault

STORY OF THE STRIPES

New rocks contain particles aligned with the Earth's magnetic field, but the field reverses every few hundred thousand years. In the 1960s, scientists studying seabed rock found matching magnetic alignments that formed paired stripes, some far apart. This showed that the seafloor had spread away from where it first formed.

◁ Fossils tell us that some far-apart lands were once joined. The mammal-like reptile *Lystrosaurus*, the freshwater reptile *Mesosaurus* and the fern *Glossopteris* have been found in southern continents that once formed one great landmass more then 200 million years ago.

Africa

South America

India

Antarctica

Australia

🐾 *Lystrosaurus*

🦌 *Mesosaurus*

🍃 *Glossopteris*

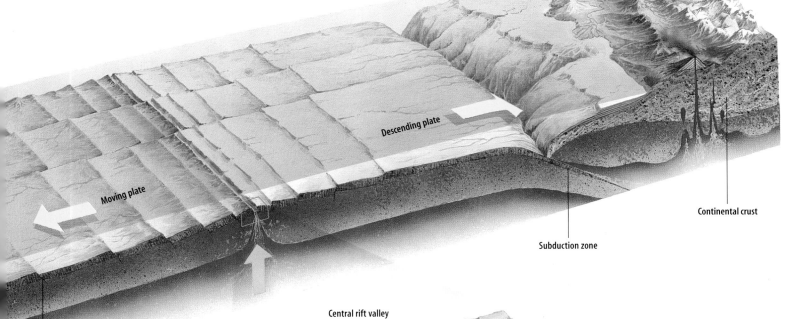

Moving plate

Descending plate

Continental crust

Subduction zone

Ocean crust

Central rift valley

Rising magma

△ New ocean floor is formed when molten crust, rising at a spreading ridge, cools and hardens. The new crust creeps outward from the ridge. A subduction zone is created when cold, dense oceanic crust sinks into the mantle below the continental crust.

◁ Magma, or molten rock, rising from the mantle builds a mid-ocean spreading ridge. Tension makes its sides crack and slip, while gravity pulls them away from the center. Unsupported, this ridge has dropped to form a rift valley.

Drowned Lands

△ Milford Sound is one of many fjords on the northwest coast of New Zealand's South Island. Fjords are narrow inlets formed when the sea invades valleys deepened by glaciers.

△ Marine archaeologists have recovered thousands of objects from the drowned city of Port Royal, Jamaica. In 1692 this port slid into the sea after an earthquake lowered the land.

S ometimes the sea invades huge tracts of low-lying land. In the past, melting ice sheets and vast undersea lava flows have caused the world's sea level to rise. One result was that parts of some continents became submerged time after time. Clues to these drowned lands are locked up in rocks. Fossils of marine animals have been found in sandstones, limestones, and shales. These rocks were formed from sediment on the seafloor but left high and dry when the land later rose or sea level fell.

Fossil evidence reveals that over 350 million years ago, prehistoric sea creatures called placoderms swam in a sea where Ohio now stands.

Fossils also show that at the end of the Cretaceous Period, 65 million years ago, a vast shallow seaway cut North America in two, while most of Europe, except for Scandinavia, lay underwater.

Some areas of low-lying land are still covered by sea today. The Bering land bridge, linking Asia and North America, was drowned by melting ice sheets around 10,000 years ago. Rising sea level has also invaded some upland coasts creating steep-sided rias and sheer-sided fjords. Elsewhere, land has sunk and some old ports have disappeared into the sea.

▽ Low tide at Cook Inlet, Alaska, exposes creeks winding through mud flats and salt marshes. Estuaries like this one are formed when a rise in sea level or a drop in land level drowns a low-lying valley.

△ The massive fossil skull of *Dunkleosteus* was discovered in Ohio. This armored sea fish grew up to 20 feet (6 m) in length. It hunted small sharks in North America's inland seas more than 350 million years ago.

▽ A variety of marine creatures lived in the long, shallow seaway that divided western and eastern North America about 65 million years ago. Reptiles included the massive turtle *Archelon* (1), mosasaurs *Clidastes* (2) and *Platecarpus* (3), and plesiosaurs *Elasmosaurus* (4) and *Trinacromerum* (5). Some hunted bony fish, such as *Xiphactinus* (6) or *Enchodus* (7). Invertebrates, such as ammonites (8) and belemnoids (9), as well as the flightless bird *Hesperonis* (10), seen here chasing the sharklike *Scapanorhynchus* (11), also lived in these waters.

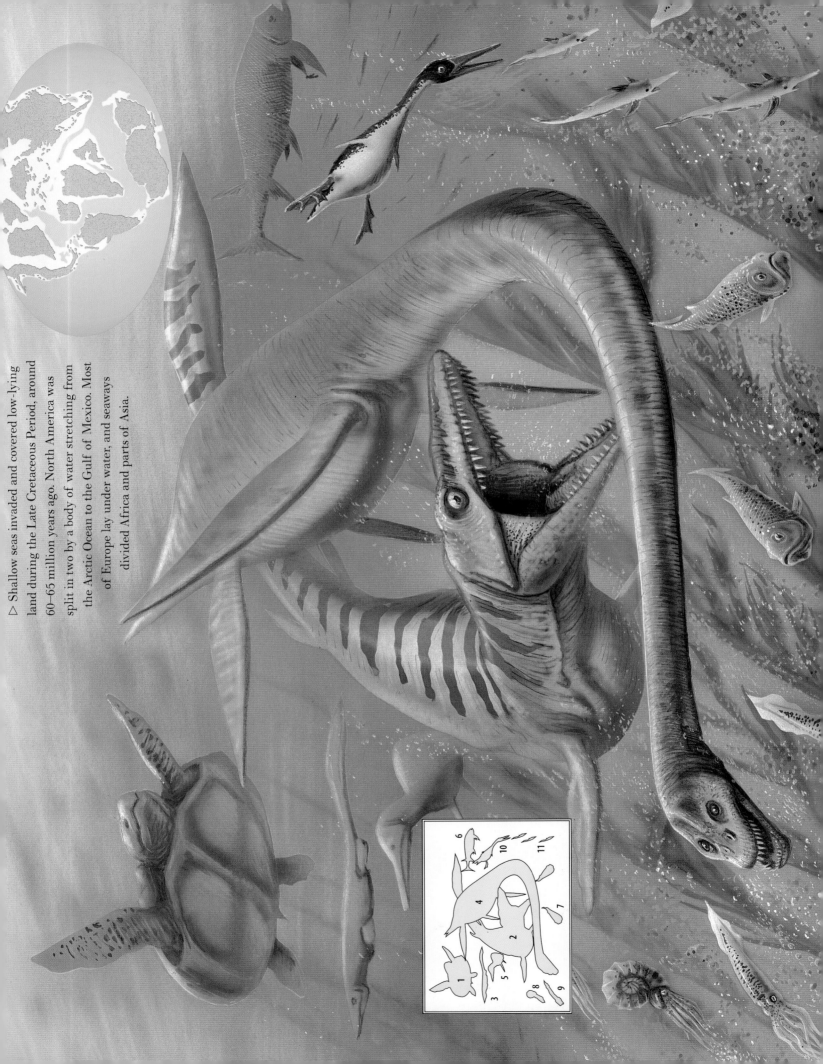

△ Shallow seas invaded and covered low-lying land during the Late Cretaceous Period, around 60–65 million years ago. North America was split in two by a body of water stretching from the Arctic Ocean to the Gulf of Mexico. Most of Europe lay under water, and seaways divided Africa and parts of Asia.

Shrunken Seas

Seas and oceans not only expand, they also shrink. About 250 million years ago, landmass collisions produced a supercontinent, Pangaea. This movement squeezed most of the shallow seas out of existence—and it might explain the world's greatest-ever mass extinction. Most creatures lived in seas that vanished. Later, colliding tectonic plates forced slabs of seabed thousands of feet above sea level. Fossil seashells have even been found on Mount Everest, the world's highest peak.

Six million years ago, rising mountains shut off the Mediterranean Sea, and dried it up. Around a million years later, the rising Atlantic Ocean broke into the Mediterranean with the greatest waterfall in Earth's history. During the last Ice Age, which ended around 10,000 years ago, so much water lay locked up in ice sheets that the world's sea level fell 300 feet (90 m). People could even walk between Asia and North America.

It is easy to spot where rising land or falling sea level has pushed a shoreline out to sea. Emergent upland coasts are visible around the Arctic, Baltic Sea, and western Scotland. Here, old sea cliffs and beaches have been left stranded high inland. Emergent lowland coasts, such as those found in the southeastern parts of the United States, feature spits, lagoons, and offshore bars.

△ Five million years ago, a massive waterfall poured over a rocky sill at the Strait of Gibraltar and refilled the Mediterranean Sea.

▽ Evaporating water leaves behind salt formations in the shrinking Dead Sea, which lies between Israel and Jordan. Similar salt deposits formed in the Mediterranean when it dried up six million years ago.

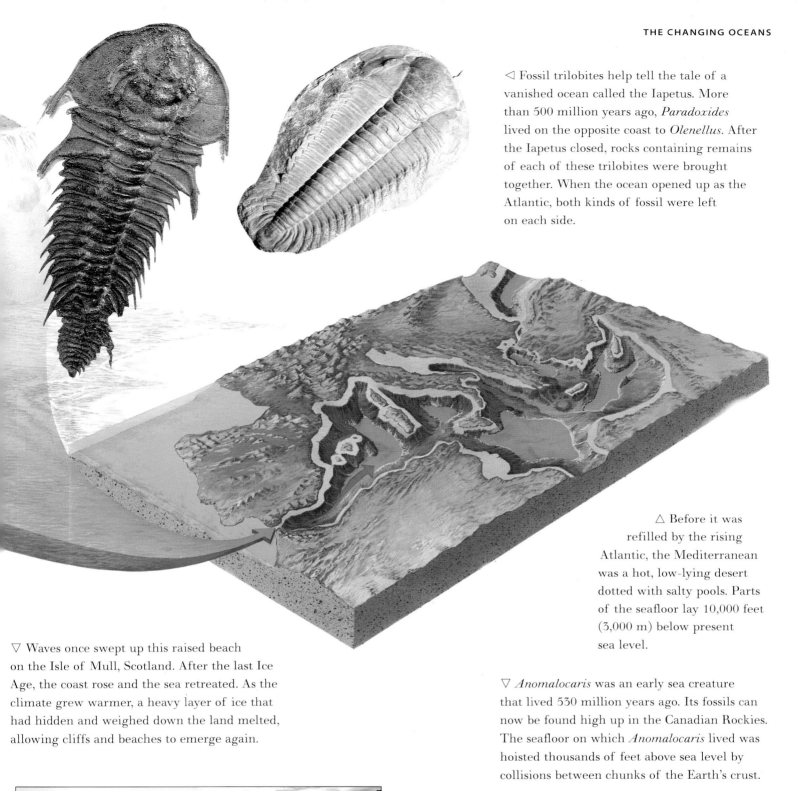

◁ Fossil trilobites help tell the tale of a vanished ocean called the Iapetus. More than 500 million years ago, *Paradoxides* lived on the opposite coast to *Olenellus*. After the Iapetus closed, rocks containing remains of each of these trilobites were brought together. When the ocean opened up as the Atlantic, both kinds of fossil were left on each side.

△ Before it was refilled by the rising Atlantic, the Mediterranean was a hot, low-lying desert dotted with salty pools. Parts of the seafloor lay 10,000 feet (3,000 m) below present sea level.

▽ Waves once swept up this raised beach on the Isle of Mull, Scotland. After the last Ice Age, the coast rose and the sea retreated. As the climate grew warmer, a heavy layer of ice that had hidden and weighed down the land melted, allowing cliffs and beaches to emerge again.

▽ *Anomalocaris* was an early sea creature that lived 530 million years ago. Its fossils can now be found high up in the Canadian Rockies. The seafloor on which *Anomalocaris* lived was hoisted thousands of feet above sea level by collisions between chunks of the Earth's crust.

The Invisible Landscape

The seafloor, or ocean basin, is a landscape as mountainous as any on dry land. The rim of this basin, known as the continental shelf, is submerged up to 590 feet (180 m). From the shelf's outer edge, the continental slope slants down at least 10,000 feet (3,000 m) to form a colossal boundary wall. Deep canyons scar this slope. Sediment settling at the foot of the slope forms the continental rise. This gentle slope ends on the seafloor. Here the abyssal plains are found. These are coated with a smooth layer of sediment. Next come ridges of abyssal hills, occupying nearly one-third of the seafloor. Beyond these rears a mid-ocean mountain range flanked by a central rift valley. Up to 6,560 feet (2,000 m) high, these ranges run through all the oceans, creating Earth's greatest mountain chain.

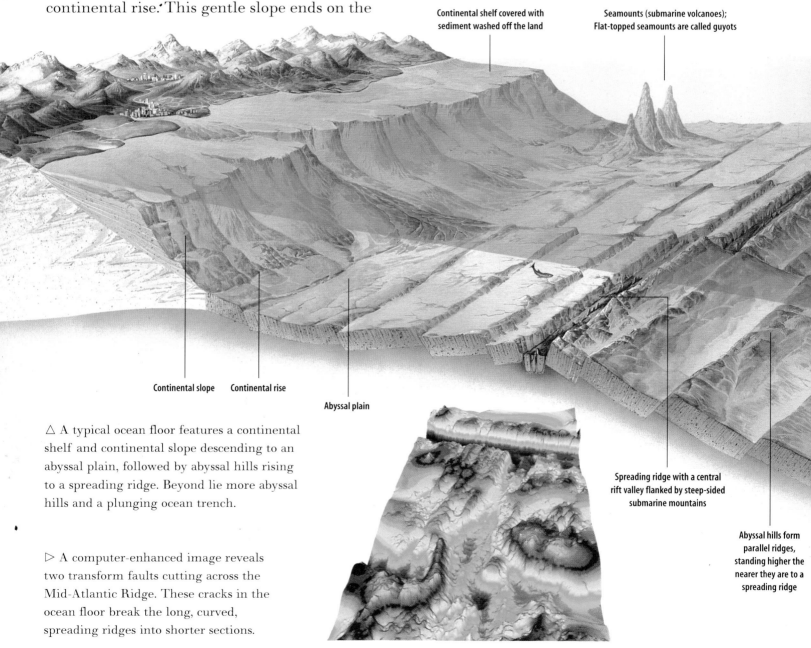

Continental shelf covered with sediment washed off the land

Seamounts (submarine volcanoes); Flat-topped seamounts are called guyots

Continental slope   Continental rise

Abyssal plain

Spreading ridge with a central rift valley flanked by steep-sided submarine mountains

Abyssal hills form parallel ridges, standing higher the nearer they are to a spreading ridge

△ A typical ocean floor features a continental shelf and continental slope descending to an abyssal plain, followed by abyssal hills rising to a spreading ridge. Beyond lie more abyssal hills and a plunging ocean trench.

▷ A computer-enhanced image reveals two transform faults cutting across the Mid-Atlantic Ridge. These cracks in the ocean floor break the long, curved, spreading ridges into shorter sections.

▷ Ocean floor sediment
includes mud and sand washed
off the land (terrigenous
deposits), dust from volcanoes
(red clay), chalky planktonic
shells (calcareous ooze), and
tiny skeletons (radiolarian
and diatom ooze).

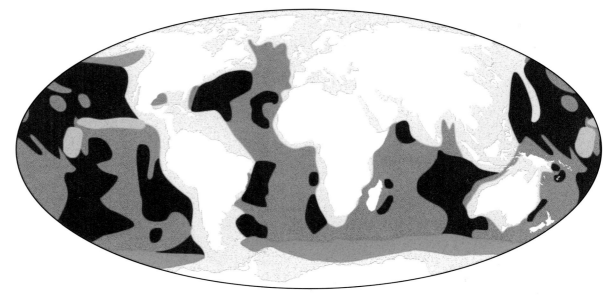

☐ *Terrigenous deposits*
▨ *Calcareous ooze*
■ *Red clay*
▧ *Radiolarian ooze*
▨ *Diatom ooze*

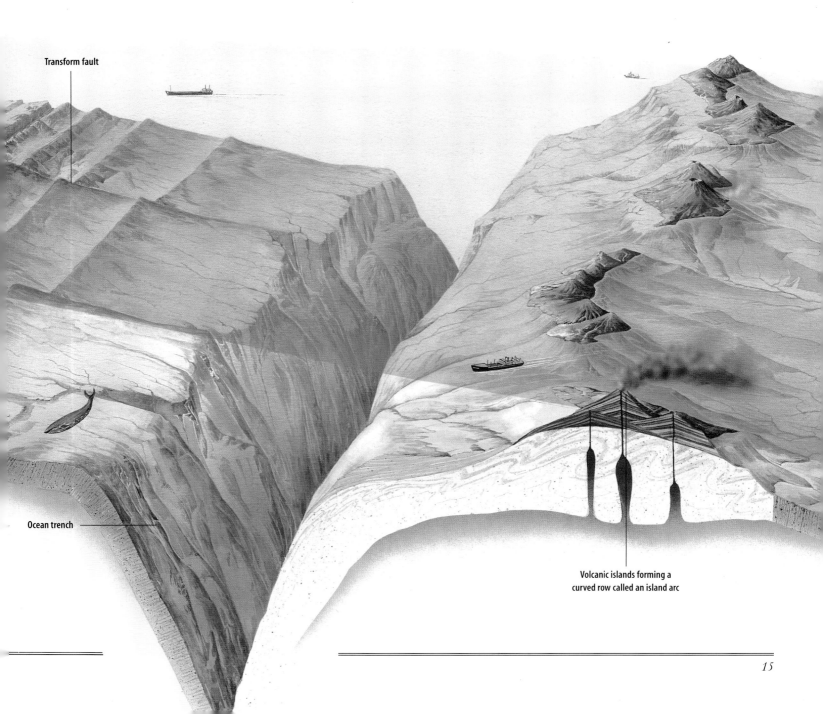

Transform fault

Ocean trench

**Volcanic islands forming a
curved row called an island arc**

15

Seamounts and Islands

Thousands of islands began as the red-hot tips of seabed volcanoes. Far out in the Atlantic Ocean, Iceland and Ascension Island formed from molten rock leaked by the Mid-Atlantic Ridge.

The Pacific Ocean and Caribbean Sea have curved rows of mountainous islands on the landward sides of ocean trenches. Here, an ocean plate and its sediment plunged into the Earth's mantle. Some of the rocks melted deep down beneath the surface. The light ingredients then rose through the mantle's dense rock, burning holes through the crust and bobbing up to build a volcanic island arc.

Volcanic islands drifting away from a hot spot sink as their weight depresses the plate they rest on. Weather erodes their exposed slopes. Then waves chop off their tops. They become the flat-capped submarine peaks called guyots. Seamounts are islands that break the surface. Some of these submarine volcanoes rise thousands of feet and still do not emerge.

▷ An atoll begins as a coral reef surrounding a volcanic island. As the island sinks, the reef grows upward. Eventually, the island disappears completely and all that remains is a ring-shaped reef, or atoll, surrounding a lagoon.

Moving plate

Loihi

Pacific Plate

Upper mantle

Stationary hot spot

△ In the Pacific Ocean, hundreds of islands formed in a straight line above a fixed hot spot in the mantle. The Hawaiian Islands emerged one by one as pulses of molten rock from a hot spot punched up through the ocean plate moving overhead. Loihi, the newest volcano in the chain, is still below sea level.

BREAKING AWAY

Not all islands spring from the oceans. Some are old parts of the mainland cut off by the sea. These islands range from tiny outcrops to large landmasses. The British Isles were once joined to the European mainland during the last Ice Age when sea level was much lower than it is now.

▽ The Aleutian Islands extend from mainland Alaska in a six hundred-mile long chain. They appeared after rock melted deep down in the Aleutian Trench, then bobbed up through the crust beyond the trench to build a curved row of volcanic islands.

◁ Surtsey Island exploded into existence following an undersea volcanic eruption in 1963. The island lies off the coast of Iceland, a country where a great deal of volcanic activity takes place. After the eruption, Surtsey Island continued to grow. Within three years, it stood 567 feet (173 m) high and covered 1.6 miles (2.6 km).

Aleutian Trench

Aleutian Islands

Seawater

The early Earth was a scorching and waterless planet. Volcanoes belched scalding steam, and water vapor hung above a mainly molten surface. Then, about 3.8 billion years ago, the temperature fell below water's boiling point and the vapor began to condense into rain. A deluge that lasted thousands of years fed rivers and filled hollows with water. Seawater began as freshwater, but minerals washed off the land soon made it salty.

▽ The Earth's water is forever going around in a circle. Water evaporates from oceans, rivers, and plants (1). The cooled water vapor condenses into droplets, forming clouds (2).

These droplets combine to fall as rain or snow (3). The water then returns in rivers and groundwater to the oceans (4). The whole process is known as the water cycle.

▷ Molten rock and flashes of lightning lit up the downpour that filled the first oceans. For thousands of years, torrents of rain fell from the clouds of steam spewed out by volcanoes.

Deep down, all ocean water is cold. The deepest water is colder than freezing, less than 30°F (-1°C), but stays liquid because it is under pressure (water pressure increases with depth). Temperature and salinity affect water density. Cold, salty water is denser, so it sinks below warmer surface water. The differences in density keep sea currents flowing.

SEAWATER COMPOSITION

Seawater is 96.5 percent pure water (the combined elements oxygen and hydrogen). Salt (the elements sodium and chlorine) make up 2.9 percent. The remaining 0.6 percent of seawater consists of various other elements.

Water 96.5 %

0.6% made up of: trace elements, calcium, fluoride, boron, bromine, bicarbonate, strontium, sulphate, magnesium and potassium

Sodium (1%)

Chlorine (1.9%)

THE CARBON CYCLE

Seawater dissolves carbon dioxide in the atmosphere. Tiny, plantlike organisms, including diatoms (shown here magnified), use the carbon for making food. Then they breathe out carbon dioxide waste, completing the carbon cycle. On the seabed, carbon in dead organisms helps to make oil and gas.

Sea Ice

North Pole

Key to Arctic map

Permanent pack ice

Maximum extent of sea ice

Key to Antarctica map

Minimum extent of sea ice

Ice shelf

Ice cap

Arctic

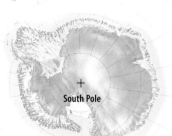

South Pole

Antarctica

Around Antarctica and in the Arctic Ocean, the seas wear a lid of ice that spreads and shrinks with the changing seasons. As the short polar summer ends, ice crystals give the sea a greasy look. This grease ice thickens into wave-shaped disks that jam together, building ice floes. Colliding ice floes make a mighty sheet of pack ice up to 16 feet (5m) thick, scarred by ridges and seamed by narrow strips of water called polynyas.

Massive icebergs also float in these polar seas. Each year, thousands of castle-shaped icebergs snap off from the glaciers of Alaska, Greenland, and Antarctica. Weighing as much as 1.5 million tons, up to 88 percent of a castle iceberg may lie under the water's surface. Flat-topped tabular icebergs come from the ice shelves that rim Antarctica. These vast icebergs are often more than 50 miles (80 km) long.

Melted by the Sun or carried by ocean currents into warmer waters, pack ice melts in summer and some icebergs shrink and disappear.

△ Ice covers most of the Arctic Ocean in winter and grips Antarctic shores even in summer. The enormous ice sheet that covers Antarctica extends over the surrounding ocean in some places, to make permanent floating ice shelves around this continent's coast.

▷ The smooth contours of a large, blue Antarctic iceberg provide a good resting place for chinstrap penguins. Sheets of water that melted and refroze produced this rare type of ice island, made of extremely strong ice with an eerily blue color.

△ Polar bears hunt on sea ice in the Arctic and off the coast of Canada. These powerful animals seize ringed seals as they bob up through breathing holes in the ice. In mild winters, bears go hungry because the sea freezes late and melts early.

▽ Castle icebergs snap off from the ends of glaciers—rivers of ice that creep down the steep-sided valleys of Greenland, Alaska, and Antarctica to the coast. This castle iceberg is melting into the ocean off Greenland.

◁ A Russian icebreaker is able to smash its way through sea ice off Antarctica. These powerful icebreakers can override and break ice 16 feet (5 m) thick by using the weight of their heavy, reinforced bows.

▷ Flat-topped tabular icebergs are found mainly in Antarctica. They are formed when massive fragments of the ice shelf break off and float away.

Rivers in the Sea

▽ In 1990, ocean currents carried toys and sneakers almost 1,500 miles (2,400 km) across the Pacific (1).

Currents flow like rivers through the sea. They are driven by winds and local differences in water density, and deflected by coasts, deep-sea ridges, and the Earth's rotation.

North and south of the Equator, surface currents circle the oceans in great loops called gyres. Warm surface currents take the Sun's heat far beyond the tropics—the tropical Gulf Stream feeds the North Atlantic Drift, which keeps Norway's Arctic coast ice-free in winter. But cold surface currents bring frigid water to places well outside polar regions.

▽ Currents on the surface flow clockwise north of the Equator, but counterclockwise around southern oceans. Cold water from the polar regions travels toward the Equator, helping to replace warm water flowing away from the tropics.

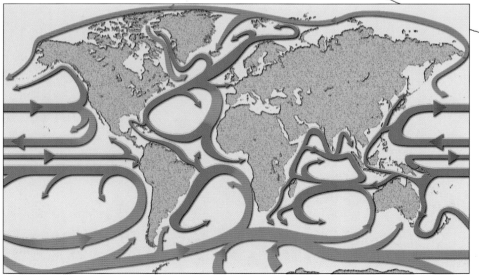

→ Cold currents
→ Warm currents

△ The Gulf Stream and the North Atlantic Drift carry tropical American seeds (2) across the Atlantic to the British Isles. Wine bottles thrown from a ship between South America and Antarctica (3) in 1977 were later recovered thousands of miles away after drifting across the Indian and Pacific oceans.

Sudden changes to an ocean current can often have huge impacts. In some years, when a warm-water flow (known as *El Niño*) displaces the cold current off Peru and Ecuador, fish catches decline and rain falls on deserts nearby.

Beneath the surface, water masses sink and flow along the ocean floor. Surface water that becomes colder and saltier than the water below it will sink, and the displaced water will rise to replace it. This process is known as thermohaline circulation. In polar regions, dense water sinks and flows along the seabed reaching far into the tropics and beyond. Eventually, this circular process exchanges top and bottom water in all the oceans.

△ Offshore winds drive surface water away from the west coasts of Africa and South America. Cold, dense, deep-level water then rises to replace the water that has been lost. This movement means different layers of water become mixed.

▽ Deep ocean currents carry dense, cold water from polar regions through ocean basins into the tropics, or beyond. Deep-sea currents travel very slowly. It can take 1,000 years for deep-level water to reappear at the surface.

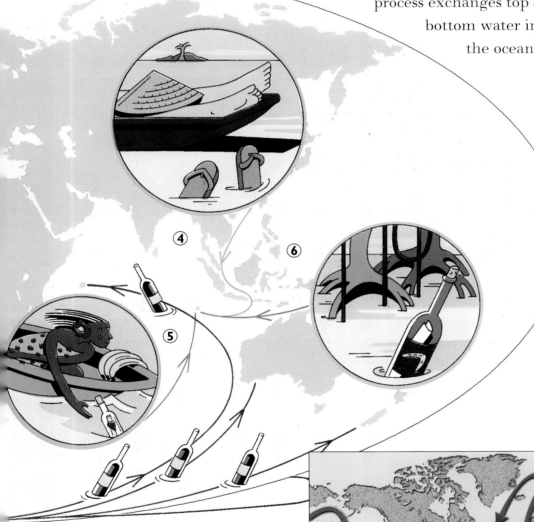

△ Ocean currents carried plastic sandals (4) from Taiwan, and bottles (5 and 6) with messages inside them from Mauritius and Australia, on a journey to the Cocos Islands in the Indian Ocean.

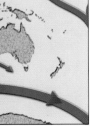

Tides

On most coasts, sea level rises and falls twice a day. The main cause of these tides is the pulling force of the Moon. Its gravitational attraction lifts the ocean surface on the side of the Earth facing the Moon. At the same time, the Earth's rotation tries to throw off water on the side of the Earth farthest from the Moon. These water bulges travel around the Earth at the same pace as the orbiting Moon, bringing high tides. In between are the troughs that cause low tides.

About twice a month, the combined pull of the Moon and the Sun creates the highest high tides and lowest low tides, called spring tides. In certain narrow bays these tides can rise higher than a house. Neap tides, with the smallest tidal range, occur between spring tides.

There are several factors that affect the behavior of tides. The Earth's rotation steers them to one side and slows them down, while coasts and seafloor ridges deflect or block them. Oceans are also divided into "tidal units." These units have a point at their center where there is no tide at all. The tidal range is greatest where waves move into shallow coastal water.

▷ Traditionally, fishermen in the Bay of Fundy, Nova Scotia, waited for low tide to collect fish that had been swept into staked nets by the high tide. The Bay of Fundy has the greatest tidal range on Earth.

△ Seawater pours through the barrage across the Rance Estuary, France. The rush of water spins turbine blades to generate electricity. Built in 1966, this was the world's first major tidal power plant.

▷ Spring tides (the highest high tides and lowest low tides) occur when the Moon and Sun line up, combining their gravitational pull. Weaker neap tides (the lowest high tides and the highest low tides) occur when the Moon and Sun pull at right angles. Spring tides happen at new and full moon. Neap tides coincide with the Moon's first and last quarters.

Spring tides

▽ At low tide (*left*), a vast sandy beach links Mont St. Michel to mainland France. At high tide, the sea turns the rock into a small island.

◁▽ The Severn Bore is a wave that travels far up the Severn River, England. A bore occurs where a high spring tide moves up a shallow estuary against river water flowing downstream.

Neap tides

Incoming tide

Tidal crest

River flow

Waves

Waves are raised by winds. A wave's size and speed depends on the wind's strength and its fetch—how far across the sea it blows. Strong, steady winds that blow across a great expanse of ocean can build huge smooth-topped waves called swells. The length between one crest and the next (the wavelength) can be over half a mile with speeds up to 35 mph (55 km/hr).

In 1933, during a North Pacific storm, a ship's officer measured a wave towering 112 feet (34.2 m) high. More than 60 years later this was still a wave height record for a storm wave. Its wavelength was nearly 1,310 feet (400 m).

Waves form rows of ridges and valleys moving through the water. Sometimes waves from two storms cross each other's path. If crest meets crest, the waves increase in size. If crest meets trough (the bottom of the wave), the waves grow smaller. Waves meeting at right angles create a choppy sea.

The biggest waves to strike a shore are seismic sea waves, or tsunamis, set off by earthquakes, landslips, or volcanoes. Nearly 7,000 years ago, a tsunami wave 1,180 feet (360 m) high swamped the Shetland Islands.

△ Floating objects in the open ocean often bob up and down on a passing wave without being carried along. Instead, the wave lifts the water particles that support the floating objects in a circular motion—up, forward, down, and back again.

▷ A huge ocean wave breaks inshore. As its crest rears up, the mass of water overbalances and starts to topple forward onto the shore.

▷ Fierce winds generate storm waves out at sea (*far right*). Hurricane-force winds can blow up to 105 mph (118 km/hr) and they may form waves more than 40 feet (13 m) high.

▽ A device installed on a windy coast is used to harness wave power. First, a wave drives air out of the chamber, spinning the turbine blades that generate electricity. Then the wave recedes, letting in more air for the next wave to force out. This air trap system has been put to effective use in Ireland and Norway.

▷ Wind-driven waves dragging on a shallow seabed slow, steepen, rise, and break. The swashing noise of the waves is the rush of water up the beach. The backwash is the return flow.

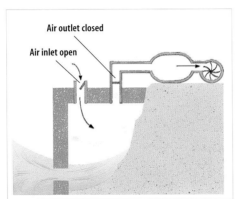

Wind direction

Trough

Crest

Breaking wave

Swash

Backwash

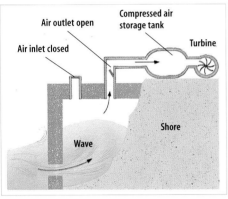

Air outlet open

Compressed air storage tank

Turbine

Air inlet closed

Shore

Wave

Air outlet closed

Air inlet open

Web of Life

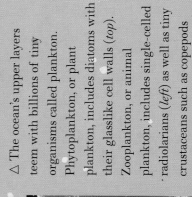

A cup of seawater teems with millions of microscopic animals and single-celled plants. These tiny organisms, known as plankton, provide food directly or indirectly for almost all the larger creatures living in the oceans.

Plant forms of plankton, or phytoplankton, use sunlight to manufacture food from chemicals in water. Animal plankton, or zooplankton, includes one-celled radiolarians, jellyfish, baby fish, and tiny crustaceans such as copepods, crab larvae, and shrimp.

Every organism in the ocean forms a link in a marine food chain and is part of a food pyramid. While zooplankton feeds on phytoplankton, both kinds are eaten by thousands of tiny fish. In turn, these feed hundreds of larger animals—enough food for just one shark or another top predator. Some food chains are simple. Krill, a kind of zooplankton, is the staple food of huge baleen whales. Other chains interlink and form complicated food webs.

△ The ocean's upper layers teem with billions of tiny organisms called plankton. Phytoplankton, or plant plankton, includes diatoms with their glasslike cell walls (top). Zooplankton, or animal plankton, includes single-celled radiolarians (left) as well as tiny crustaceans such as copepods (right) and crab larvae (center).

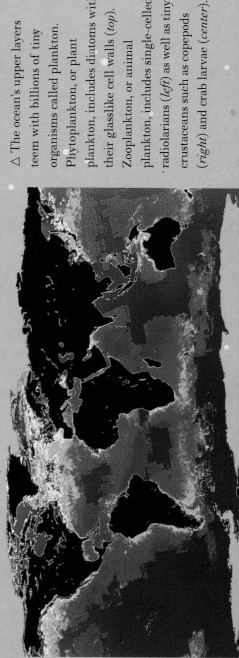

△ The distribution of plant plankton, or phytoplankton, varies as this satellite image shows. The red areas are the richest in plankton, followed by yellow, green, blue, and violet, the least dense. Gray areas indicate where there is a lack of information. This picture was taken during the spring when phytoplankton is most plentiful.

△▽ All life in the sea is linked together in a vast and complex food web. Over 90 percent of marine creatures are eaten by larger and more powerful species. Plankton provide the basis for this system.

▽ Droppings and dead organisms from the upper levels of the ocean sink to the lower depths. Here, they provide nourishment for life on the seabed. Bacteria also break down the remains into nutrients and minerals. Upwellings carry these back to the surface where the food cycle begins again.

Fish

Sea fish are superbly adapted to life in the oceans. Their gills breathe oxygen dissolved in water. Most swim with powerful sweeps of the tail, steering and braking with fins. Nostrils, eyes, and vibration-sensitive cells on their flanks warn them of prey and predators.

Prey fish use various methods to avoid being eaten. Sardines swim in shoals for protection, their dark backs and pale bellies providing camouflage when viewed from above or below. If chased, flying fish leap from the sea and glide on winglike fins.

The great majority of the 20,000 different species of fish are bony fish. They have special bladders controlling the level at which they swim. Bony fish include tuna, sardines, flatfish such as flounder and sole, and sailfish—the world's fastest fish, which can reach speeds of up to 60 mph (100 km/hr).

The 600 cartilaginous, or gristly, kinds of fish include torpedo-shaped sharks and flat rays. Cartilaginous fish tend to sink unless they keep swimming.

△ The great white shark, the largest carnivorous fish, can weigh more than 1.5 tons. Some may grow to more than 20 feet (6 m) in length.

Herring

Pike

Flying fish

Piranha

Catfish

△ The distinctively-shaped ocean sunfish, or mola mola, appears to have more head than body. Weighing two tons or more, this weak swimmer is the heaviest of all bony fish.

△ A spiny "mane" gives the lionfish of the Indian and Pacific oceans its name. Its hollow spines are poisonous.

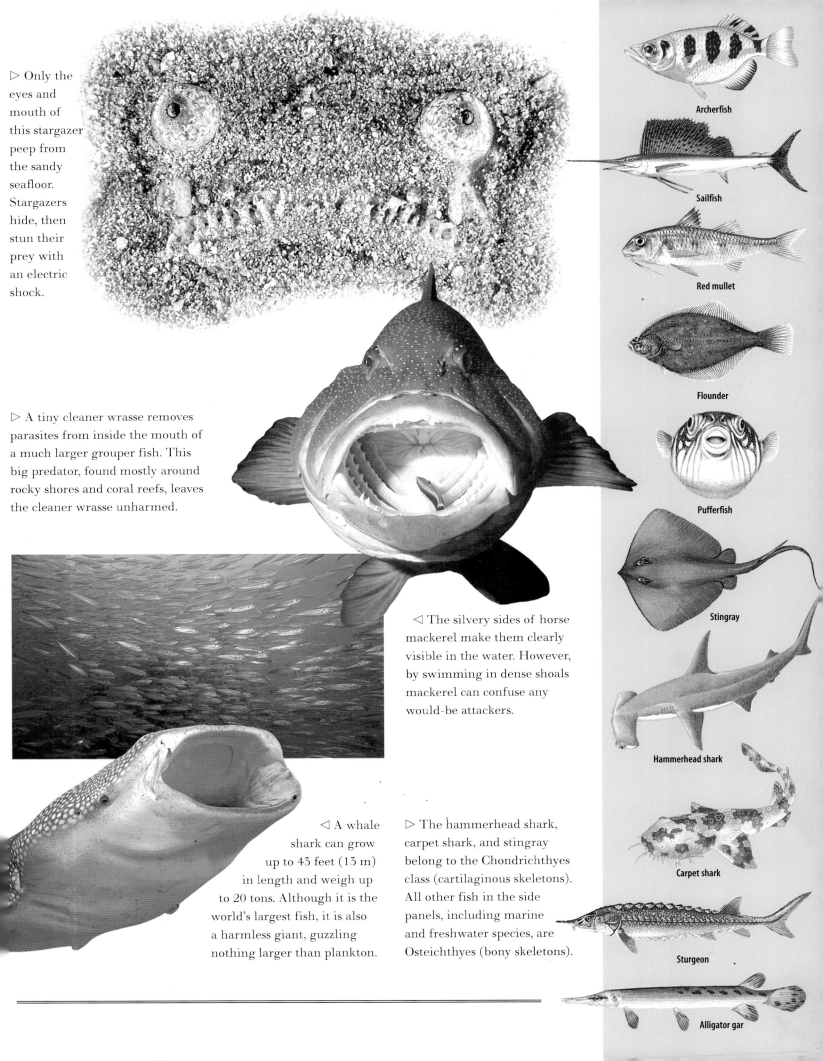

▷ Only the eyes and mouth of this stargazer peep from the sandy seafloor. Stargazers hide, then stun their prey with an electric shock.

▷ A tiny cleaner wrasse removes parasites from inside the mouth of a much larger grouper fish. This big predator, found mostly around rocky shores and coral reefs, leaves the cleaner wrasse unharmed.

◁ The silvery sides of horse mackerel make them clearly visible in the water. However, by swimming in dense shoals mackerel can confuse any would-be attackers.

◁ A whale shark can grow up to 43 feet (13 m) in length and weigh up to 20 tons. Although it is the world's largest fish, it is also a harmless giant, guzzling nothing larger than plankton.

▷ The hammerhead shark, carpet shark, and stingray belong to the Chondrichthyes class (cartilaginous skeletons). All other fish in the side panels, including marine and freshwater species, are Osteichthyes (bony skeletons).

Archerfish

Sailfish

Red mullet

Flounder

Pufferfish

Stingray

Hammerhead shark

Carpet shark

Sturgeon

Alligator gar

Sea Mammals

Mammals are warm-blooded creatures that cannot breathe under water, yet millions of years ago some took to the sea to find food. Their descendants developed into expert swimmers, with flipper-shaped limbs and thick body fat to protect them against the deadly cold of the water.

Seals, sea lions, and walruses are graceful swimmers in water, but clumsy movers on land. Most come ashore only to breed or rest. Other sea mammals, such as sea cows and whales, cannot leave the sea at all, although their ancestors could. In 1994, scientists discovered the 50 million year old fossil of *Ambulocetus*, a small whale with hind legs.

Whales either have teeth or whalebone (baleen) plates. Toothed whales mainly hunt fish or squid, although killer whales seize penguins, seals, and even other whales. A baleen whale's plates trap tiny fish or plankton when it squirts out a mouthful of water. Baleens include the blue whale—the largest of all animals.

△ Male northern elephant seals fight for control of a beach. A victorious male mates with the females on the beach he controls.

▽ Manatees are distantly related to elephants. Their paddle-shaped forelimbs and flat tails makes them powerful swimmers. Manatees never come ashore. They eat plants growing in warm, shallow Atlantic waters and rivers.

▽ Walruses use their snouts rather than their tusks to dig clams from the seabed. Males can grow to over 10 feet (3 m) in length and weigh around 2,600 pounds (1,200 kg).

△ Sperm whales are toothed whales up to 65 feet (20 m) in length and weighing up to 70 tons. Males can dive 9,800 feet (3,000 m) to hunt squid on the seabed, and stay down for nearly two hours.

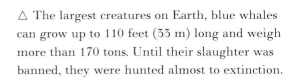

△ The largest creatures on Earth, blue whales can grow up to 110 feet (33 m) long and weigh more than 170 tons. Until their slaughter was banned, they were hunted almost to extinction.

▽ Sea otters eat and sleep on their backs. They swim off North Pacific coasts and feed on crabs, clams, fish, and mussels. A sea otter often uses its front paws to grasp a shellfish and smash it open against a rock balanced on its belly.

◁ Bottle-nosed dolphins are small, fast, toothed whales with fishlike fins and flippers. These graceful creatures hunt fish in warm or tropical waters around the world.

△ The streamlined bodies of California sea lions make them very agile in the water. They hunt for fish among the kelp forests off the west coast of North America.

Coral Reefs

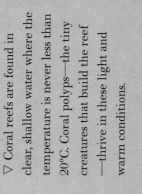

Coral reefs are found in warm, shallow seas and oceans. A reef is made up from billions of little stony cups, most no bigger than a thumbnail. Each cup once hid a tiny coral polyp, a creature related to sea anemones and jellyfish. When the polyp dies, it leaves behind a hard, outer skeleton over which new polyps begin to grow. Colonies of living polyps create green, purple, orange, and yellow corals shaped like crusts, brains, branches, fans, or stags' horns.

Coral reefs support a huge variety of life. Sponges, sea anemones, lionfish, sea slugs, and predators such as sea snakes, groupers, and barracudas are just a few of the reef's many inhabitants. In fact, one-third of all fish species can be found on coral reefs.

The reef provides each creature with a plentiful food supply. Sponges suck in tiny organisms, and sea anemones paralyze and eat small fish. Butterflyfish probe coral heads for crustaceans and mollusks. Certain creatures, such as the crown-of-thorns starfish, feed on the coral itself.

▽ Coral reefs are found in clear, shallow water where the temperature is never less than 20°C. Coral polyps—the tiny creatures that build the reef —thrive in these light and warm conditions.

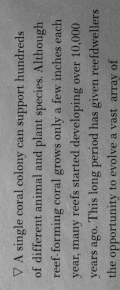

▽ A single coral colony can support hundreds of different animal and plant species. Although reef-forming coral grows only a few inches each year, many reefs started developing over 10,000 years ago. This long period has given reefdwellers the opportunity to evolve a vast array of

▽ Creatures of the coral reef include the sea turtle (1), the manta ray (2), and lionfish (3), which has deadly poisonous spines. The brilliant colors of the sea snail (4), nudibranch (5), and starfish (6) make them stand out against the other species. Top predators, such as the grouper (7) and sea snake (8), live among the sponges (9) and corals (10). The coral-eating crown-of-thorns starfish

Life in the Depths

Most sea creatures depend on plantlike phytoplankton for their food supply, but not much of this can flourish in the dim light below 590 feet (180 m). Creatures of the twilight zone (490–3,280 feet/1,000 m deep) eat one another, or survive on dead animals and algae that rain down from above. Some swim up to feed at night, camouflaged by darkness. Down here, sharks find prey by scent or vibrations set off by their prey's bodies. Other inhabitants include swarms of squid, shrimp, prawns, and billions of deep-sea copepods.

Black bodies conceal some fish from their enemies at these levels. Lanternfish and hatchet fish, however, glow with little lights or shine with silvery, reflective sides to confuse their predators.

No light penetrates below 3,280 feet (1,000 m). Small, flabby fish live here, such as viperfish and gulper eels with fanged jaws and elastic stomachs for the rare big meals that come their way. Few of these ferocious-looking deep-sea fish are more than 12 inches (30 cm) long—a larger fish would not find enough food to survive.

▽ The various species that survive in the depths of the ocean are rarely more than 12 inches (30 cm) long. Some live deeper than others, and several swim to the surface at night. Many have developed special adaptations to survive in this extreme environment. The viperfish (1) and lanternfish (2) have light organs on their bodies to confuse their enemies. Others such as the anglerfish (3) and stomiatoid (4) use luminous lures to attract prey. Male anglerfish sometimes attach themselves to the much larger female anglerfish (5) and live there permanently. The vicious teeth of the fangtooth (6) earn this hunter its name, while the pelicanlike mouth of the gulper eel (7) is almost a quarter the length of its body.

△ An expandable stomach and hinged mouth allows the deep-sea swallower to devour prey larger than itself.

▽ The razor-sharp fangs of the viperfish make it an effective predator. Like many deep-sea fish, the viperfish swims open-jawed, catching any prey between its sharp teeth before swallowing.

The Ocean Floor

More than 10,000 feet (3,000 m) down, certain seafloor creatures thrive in extremely harsh conditions—soft mud, total darkness, and colossal, water pressure. Above the seabed, sea snails and flimsy-bodied fish such as grenadiers swim around in the near-freezing water. Sea spiders and tripod fish rest or move on the muddy seabed.

Tethered to the ocean floor, glass sponges, sea squirts, sea anemones, sea lilies, and sea pens filter particles of food from the water. Burrowing worms, crustaceans, and sea cucumbers guzzle seabed ooze for hidden scraps of food.

On parts of spreading ridges, 8,200 feet (2,500 m) down and more, molten rock heats water seeping down through seabed cracks. Clouds of scalding water, dark with dissolved minerals, spurt up through seabed vents, building chimneys called black smokers. The sulphur-rich water nourishes bacteria—in turn a source of food for giant clams and tube worms, some growing nearly 3 feet (1 m) each year. These communities, first discovered in 1977, show that not all food chains depend on plants.

▷ Rocky chimneys near a spreading ridge, 8,200 feet (2,500 m) below the surface, spew out scalding water, black with mineral-rich mud. The minerals nourish bacteria, providing food for the giant clams, tube worms, and other creatures that live around black smokers.

△ A grenadier uses its fleshy, beardlike barbels to detect small creatures. The largest grenadiers grow to almost 3 feet (1 m) in length.

▽ The sea spider is found at depths of up to 16,400 feet (5,000 m). Deep-water spiders have no eyes and can measure up to 2 feet (60 cm) across.

◁ In 1995 the Japanese unmanned research submersible *Kaiko* descended almost 36,000 feet (11,000 m) into the Mariana Trench. *Kaiko* found shrimp, sea cucumbers, and jellyfish living on the deepest seafloor on Earth.

▽ The tripod fish can rest on the seabed, detecting food odors wafted by currents. Specially adapted fins stop it sinking into the soft, muddy ooze.

▽ At up to 14 inches (34 cm) in length, *Alicella gigantea* is the world's largest amphipod (a type of crustacean that is related to shrimp). It has been discovered in the deepest ocean trenches.

Seabirds

△ The wandering albatross soars on wings that have a span of up to 12 feet (3.6 m).

Hundreds of kinds of birds feed or fly at sea. Sanderlings, oystercatchers, herons, and other long-legged wading birds patrol the shore itself. Cormorants, pelicans, sea ducks, terns, and many gulls find food along inshore waters. Auks, frigate birds, gannets, and penguins range through offshore waters, while albatrosses, petrels, and shearwaters adventure far out into the open ocean.

Many seabirds have distinctive wings and styles of flight. Stubby-winged puffins whirr along with rapid wingbeats. Albatrosses' long, narrow wings enable them to glide for hours. Penguins, with wings reduced to flippers, cannot fly at all.

Most seabirds dive or swim for food. Terns dip briefly into the sea to seize their prey. Cormorants, gannets, brown pelicans, and penguins plunge in. Below the surface, cormorants swim swiftly by kicking water back with webbed feet. Little wading birds called phalaropes spin around to draw up plankton.

Each seabird has a beak to suit its way of feeding. Phalaropes' needle-shaped beaks are designed to snap up tiny organisms. Other adaptations include thick body fat and oily plumage to keep the birds warm and dry in chilly water.

△ The puffin is a stocky seabird found in the North Pacific, North Atlantic, and Arctic Ocean. Puffins are agile swimmers and can seize up to 30 sand eels at a time in their large, brightly colored beaks.

△ Special glands allow this fulmar to drink seawater without causing it any harm. The salt is filtered out through a bony nostril. Seabirds with this special adaptation are known as tubenoses.

▽ The brown pelican flies around the coasts of North and South America. It feeds on fish swimming near the surface. After diving down into the water, the pelican uses the large pouch on the underside of its bill to scoop up prey.

△ Macaroni penguins, like other penguins, cannot fly. They use their wings to rapidly propel themselves underwater. Feet and tails help them to steer. This penguin is named after the macaroni-like feathers on its head.

△ A great frigate bird chases a tropic bird. Frigate birds follow and tweak the tails of other seabirds, forcing them to drop fish intended for their young. These pirates of the air then snap up the meal for themselves.

▷ Huge colonies of gannets breed on sea cliffs and rocky islands, safe from predators such as rats and foxes. These nosiy birds feed on shoals of herring and mackerel. To catch them, gannets make spectacular dives at speeds of up to 100 mph (160 km/hr).

▽ Wilson's storm petrels flutter, glide, and sometimes patter along the surface of the sea to collect food. Their diet consists mainly of plankton and small crustaceans. Wilson's storm petrels, like many other seabirds, are sometimes driven far inland by storms at sea.

Mysteries of Migration

Every two to three years, female green turtles leave their feeding grounds off Brazil and travel back to Ascension Island, out in the Atlantic Ocean, where they were born. Here, they lay their eggs before returning across the sea again. They might navigate this 1,250-mile (2,000 km) journey by using currents, seamounts, or the Earth's magnetic field. Their two-way journey is just one of many sea migrations made by creatures traveling in search of food, breeding grounds, or safety.

△ Monarch butterflies migrate south in winter across the North American mainland to Mexico. However, strong winds blow some of them far out into the Atlantic Ocean.

△ The Arctic tern travels farther than any other bird. Some Arctic terns fly more than 21,000 miles (35,000 km) in a year, from the Arctic to the Antarctic and back.

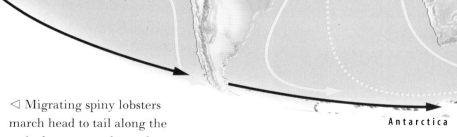

Arctic Ocean

North America

Europe

Africa

Pacific Ocean

Atlantic Ocean

South America

Antarctica

◁ Migrating spiny lobsters march head to tail along the seabed to protect themselves from enemies.

▷ An Atlantic salmon leaps a waterfall on its journey back upstream. Some adults travel thousands of miles to breed in the river where they were hatched.

42

Some journeys are quite short—squid, shrimp, and fish swim up at night from the sea's middle depths to feed on zooplankton at the surface. Other journeys are immense. Grey whales swim more than 13,600 miles (22,000 km) a year between their Arctic feeding grounds and their breeding grounds off California. Arctic terns, the champion long-distance flyers, commute between the Arctic and Antarctic regions and enjoy two summers every year.

A few return migrations happen only once a lifetime. Salmon hatch in streams but mature at sea, returning to their streams to spawn and die.

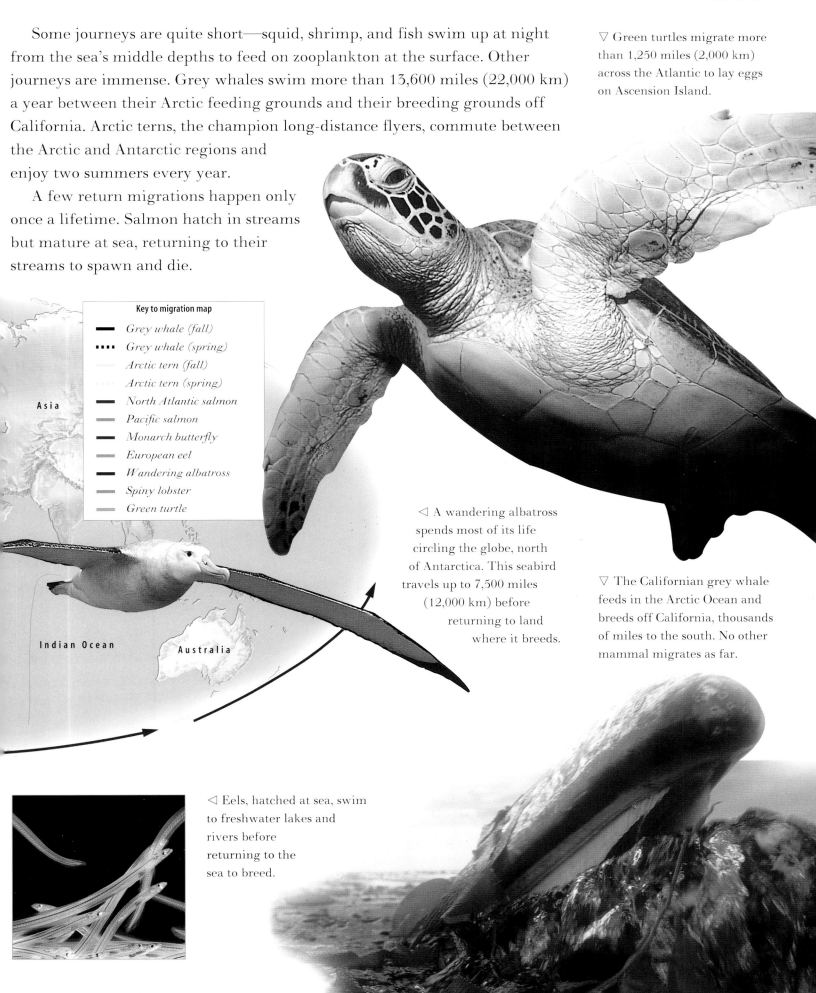

▽ Green turtles migrate more than 1,250 miles (2,000 km) across the Atlantic to lay eggs on Ascension Island.

Key to migration map

— *Grey whale (fall)*
···· *Grey whale (spring)*
— *Arctic tern (fall)*
···· *Arctic tern (spring)*
— *North Atlantic salmon*
— *Pacific salmon*
— *Monarch butterfly*
— *European eel*
— *Wandering albatross*
— *Spiny lobster*
— *Green turtle*

Asia

Indian Ocean

Australia

◁ A wandering albatross spends most of its life circling the globe, north of Antarctica. This seabird travels up to 7,500 miles (12,000 km) before returning to land where it breeds.

▽ The Californian grey whale feeds in the Arctic Ocean and breeds off California, thousands of miles to the south. No other mammal migrates as far.

◁ Eels, hatched at sea, swim to freshwater lakes and rivers before returning to the sea to breed.

Rocky Shores

Where the sea meets the land, either might gain the upper hand. In some places the land thrusts out into the sea. Elsewhere the sea eats into the land. Storm waves can undermine a sloping coast until its top tumbles and it becomes a wave-washed boulder beach backed by a retreating sea cliff.

Rocky shores are battered by storm waves and drowned by high tides. They bake in the heat and almost freeze during cold spells. Organisms found on rocky shores have evolved to survive and make the most of the conditions.

Water buoys up the fronds of seaweed while their rootlike holdfasts prevent waves from wrenching them off the rocks. Sea squirts, sponges, sea anemones, acorn barnacles, and mussels also attach themselves to rocks. They eat scraps of food washed in with the tide. Limpets and top shells graze algae growing on the boulders, while dog whelks bore holes in fellow mollusks' shells and eat their flesh. At low tide, the shells of acorn barnacles and limpets keep them safe from predators and ensure their insides remain moist.

Tide pools hold water even at low tide. Crustaceans, such as shrimp and crabs, ferocious ragworms, starfish, and small fish all find food and hiding places here.

△ Some tide pools have sandy floors. Marine creatures such as this common shrimp can burrow into the sand to avoid predators.

◁ Over time, the endless pounding of waves has cut an arch through Gaada Stack in the Shetland Islands, north of Scotland's mainland. The sea is the main cause of coastal erosion.

△ Toppled boulders litter the shore around a rocky beach at Pondfield Cove in Dorset, England. Tide pools, along with cracks and crevices in rocks and caves, provide a home for a large variety of creatures.

◁ Pencil urchins have long, broad spines with sharp ends. Slender tube feet with strong suckers drag it along and hold it in place. The urchin's mouth is below the middle of its body.

◁ The sea cucumber is related to starfish and sea urchins. It can grow up to 12 inches (30 cm) long. At low tide it can wedge itself into rock crevices. When a sea cucumber is threatened, it squirts out sticky threads to entangle an attacker.

▽ Rootlike holdfasts anchor this brown seaweed to a rock. The flexible fronds extending from the holdfasts prevent the seaweed from being ripped apart by the waves.

▽ A beadlet anemone's sticky base keeps it firmly attached to hard surfaces. Stinging cells in its tentacles stun small prey. At low tide, or when threatened, anemones withdraw their tentacles back into their bodies.

◁ Shells protect common limpets against enemies and drying out. At high tide they search for seaweed on rocks. After feeding, limpets always return to the same spot.

Sand and Pebbles

Pebbly and sandy beaches often form gently shelving shores. Pebbles are stones that have broken off a rocky coast and been rubbed smooth against one another by waves. Most sand grains are specks of ground-down pebbles. Waves coming ashore at an angle drive pebbles and sand along a coast, sort them into sizes, and then drop them in sheltered waters where they accumulate and form beaches. Bay-head beaches develop between headlands (cliffs jutting out into the sea). Others include lowland beaches backed by dunes, bars (offshore beaches), and spits (beaches growing out into the sea).

Few organisms can survive the crushing force of stones rolled up and down a pebble beach by waves. A sandy beach also poses problems.

▷ This gently sloping beach in California was built from eroded sea cliff ground down by the sea. Wind-driven waves have carried and piled up pebbles along the water's edge.

△ Cockles are heart-shaped bivalves—mollusks with a shell of two hinged halves. Cockles burrow and move around using a muscular foot.

▽ Razor shells are long, narrow bivalves that bury themselves in the sand. At high tide their feeding tubes poke above the sand to suck in plankton carried in by the water.

◁ Winds have shifted sand and built up dunes behind this beach in Scotland. Marram grass, rooted in the loose sand, helps to fix the dunes in place.

The sand dries out in the sun, shifts in storms and lacks rocks for animals to grip or hide beneath. Even so, millions of burrowing creatures find safety a few inches underneath the surface of a sandy beach.

At low tide, tiny pits and bumps betray an invisible army of worms, mollusks, crabs, shrimp, echinoderms, such as heart urchins and sand stars. At high tide, some burrowers climb out and swim or crawl in search of food. Others stay put and suck in plankton through feeding tubes, or poke out tentacles to capture passing morsels. Lugworms remain buried, extracting nourishment from muddy sand.

Even burrowing does not always give protection to small inhabitants of sandy shores. At high tide, fish swim inshore to snap up the unwary. At low tide, wading birds with long, sensitive beaks pry molluscs from their crumbly caves.

◁ Grunions lay their eggs on the beaches of southern California between February and September. These small fish wait until night, when very high tides sweep them up onto the sandy shores.

▽ A lugworm (*left*) sucks in sand containing scraps of food and squirts out waste in coils. At low tide, a hole betrays its burrow on the beach.

▷ When a masked crab burrows in the sand, it draws water through its long tube antennae. At high tide it crawls out of the sand to feed.

Muddy Shores

When sluggish rivers dump sediment in bays and estuaries, land grows out into the sea. In quiet coastal waters, tiny particles of mud form small islands where water plants take root, despite the surge of the tides. Mud lodging on plant stems enlarges these islands. They grow higher and broader, eventually forming a salt marsh. Deltas and tropical mangrove swamps also form where mud or silt builds land into the sea.

Only certain burrowing creatures can tolerate these places, where closely packed particles of mud block breathing tubes and fresh-water flowing downstream replaces salt water when the tide turns. Mud-dwelling specialists include soft-shelled clams called gapers, sea mice (small, hairy worms), minute hydrobia snails, cockles, whelks, amphipods and peacock worms. Between them, they filter mud for plant remains, suck microscopic organisms from the water, and eat other small creatures.

▽ Mudskippers are fish that can breathe air and use finlike "elbows" to hop around mangrove swamp shores at low tide.

△ Peacock worms lie buried in the mud until high tide when they poke out feathery tentacles to trap tiny food particles.

▷ Ten square feet (1 sq m) of a muddy shore can contain up to 40,000 spire shells. These tiny snails eat plankton washed in with the tide.

◁ The crab-eating macaque lives in mangrove forests. For food, it comes down from the trees and forages for crabs and mollusks at the water's edge.

△ The mangrove snake is an agile tree climber and is often found among the branches that overhang water. At night, mangrove snakes hunt birds, frogs, and small mammals.

△ Beneath a sea mouse's outer protection of spines, a mat of hairs keeps mud from clogging up its breathing system. This small sea worm burrows in muddy sand, feeding on dead matter.

▽ A male fiddler crab waves its front claw to attract a mate or to menace another male. Fiddler crabs live in burrows dug in muddy beaches. They feed on a mixture of mud and algae.

△ Stiltlike roots anchor mangrove trees to the wet, salty mud along tropical shorelines. The roots help build up dry land by slowing down the current and catching hold of dirt and sand. Many marine creatures live among the roots.

Island Life

Animals and plants reach islands in various ways. Some were already living on land that became separated from the mainland. Small bats, birds, and insects can be blown out to remote ocean islands on storm winds. Birds bring plant seeds, and ocean currents deliver drifting fruit. Clumps of floating vegetation are washed out to sea by rivers and carried to islands on the tide. They sometimes carry insects, mollusks, reptiles and even mammals.

In time, island animals evolve differently from their mainland ancestors. Many flies, moths, and birds develop shrunken wings and lose the power to fly. This saves them from being blown out to sea and drowned. On the Indonesian island of Celebes, dwarf buffaloes evolved from a much larger species. This allows them to survive on the limited food supplies.

Small animals may also become giants on islands where there are no predators to keep their numbers down. Rats the size of dogs once lived on Mediterranean islands. The giant crabs and huge tortoises that are found on islands in the Pacific and Indian oceans evolved from much smaller creatures.

▷ The ring-tailed lemur is a relative of the monkey. Dozens of lemur species evolved on Madagascar after the island was cut off from Africa. Lemurs are not found anywhere else.

▽ Marine iguanas evolved from lizards stranded long ago on the Galapagos Islands off South America. Unlike other iguanas, they have adapted to feeding in the sea.

◁ Some of the ancestors of creatures now living on the Galapagos Islands were carried on driftwood or flew there. A remarkable variety of animals has adapted to survive on these isolated islands in the Pacific Ocean. They include sharp-clawed marine iguanas, flightless cormorants with shrunken wings, giant tortoises, and scarlet crabs.

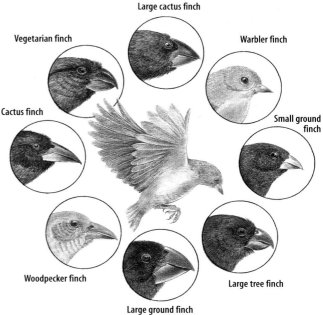

Large cactus finch

Vegetarian finch

Warbler finch

Cactus finch

Small ground finch

Woodpecker finch

Large tree finch

Large ground finch

△ Darwin's finches all evolved from one ancestral species marooned on the Galapagos Islands. Each bird has a different beak shape suited to a particular diet. Some eat seeds, and others eat insects or fruit. This ensures that the limited food supplies are not exhausted.

▽ The dodo, a flightless bird with no enemies, once flourished on the island of Mauritius in the Indian Ocean. However, by 1700 it had been wiped out by the humans, dogs, and rats that arrived on the island from Europe.

Early Ocean Explorers

△ *Brendan*, an ox-hide boat, was sailed from Ireland to Newfoundland by the British adventurer Tim Severin in 1976. Old Irish writings hint that an Irish monk reached North America in a boat made from animal skins in about A.D. 570. Severin's expedition proved it was possible to make this voyage in a similar boat.

Tens of thousands of years ago, people were making sea crossings by canoe or raft to settle empty continents. The Old Stone Age ancestors of Australia's Aborigines arrived by sea from Southeast Asia at least 60,000 years ago.

From about 3000 B.C. Micronesian, Melanesian, and Polynesian seafarers began to discover the islands of the South Pacific. By A.D. 1000 the Polynesians, the greatest of these early ocean explorers, had settled all the major islands lying in the area bounded by Hawaii, New Zealand, and Easter Island. These islands form the tips of a vast triangle covering almost 8 million square miles (20 million sq km).

Farther west, Bronze Age traders and explorers were making daring voyages in fragile sailing ships. Reed ships probably traded across the Arabian Sea 4,300 years ago. A thousand years later, wooden cargo ships sailed the Mediterranean carrying precious goods such as gold, ostrich eggs, and ivory.

Experts disagree about which navigator first reached North America. Vikings had sailed to Newfoundland from Greenland by A.D. 1000. However, it is also possible that Chinese sailors, ancient Egyptians, or an Irish monk may have set foot in North America much earlier.

◁ Norsemen were Europe's greatest seafarers during the early Middle Ages. From about A.D. 800–1000, their oared sailing ships carried Viking sea raiders and traders from Scandinavia around Europe and far up its rivers. Norse settlers also crossed the Atlantic, reaching Greenland, Iceland, and Newfoundland.

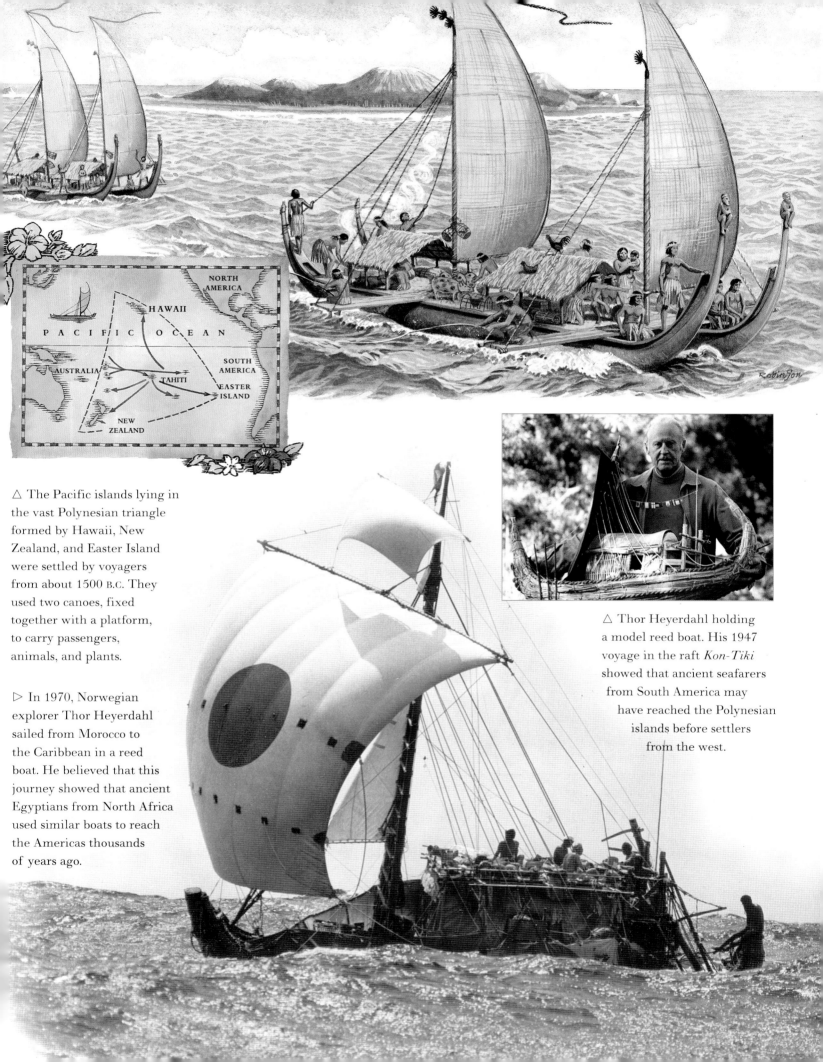

△ The Pacific islands lying in the vast Polynesian triangle formed by Hawaii, New Zealand, and Easter Island were settled by voyagers from about 1500 B.C. They used two canoes, fixed together with a platform, to carry passengers, animals, and plants.

▷ In 1970, Norwegian explorer Thor Heyerdahl sailed from Morocco to the Caribbean in a reed boat. He believed that this journey showed that ancient Egyptians from North Africa used similar boats to reach the Americas thousands of years ago.

△ Thor Heyerdahl holding a model reed boat. His 1947 voyage in the raft *Kon-Tiki* showed that ancient seafarers from South America may have reached the Polynesian islands before settlers from the west.

The Age of Exploration

▽ These modern replicas of Christopher Columbus's ships *Santa Maria*, *Niña* and *Pinta* set sail from Spain in 1992. Five hundred years earlier, Columbus's fleet of three ships, sponsored by Queen Isabella of Spain, crossed the Atlantic and reached the Bahamas.

Five centuries ago, sailors from Europe began crisscrossing the oceans and exploring the world. In the 1400s, improved navigation aids and new sailing ships, called caravels and carracks, gave European navigators the confidence to sail far beyond the sight of land. First, Portugal sent caravels down the west coast of Africa to bypass hostile Mediterranean powers and find a new sea route to the spice-rich lands of India and Southeast Asia. By 1488, Bartholomew Dias had rounded the tip of southern Africa, and by 1499, Vasco da Gama had sailed to India and back.

△ Henry the Navigator (1394–1460) played a major part in starting off the great age of ocean exploration by European seafarers. This Portugese prince organized and sent out 50 naval expeditions. Many explored the west coast of Africa as far south as Sierra Leone.

Soon Spain was competing with Portugal for Asian trade. In 1492, Christopher Columbus sailed west to seek a transatlantic route to Asia on behalf of the Spanish crown. Instead he found the islands of the Caribbean, marking the start of Spain's conquest of the Americas. In 1519, Ferdinand Magellan led a three-year Spanish expedition which became the first to circumnavigate the world and prove that it was round. But war, disease, and shipwreck took its toll—of the five ships and 241 men who set out, only the *Victoria* and 19 men returned.

Little by little such journeys helped cartographers to map the edges of the oceans. Major discoveries were still being made in the 1700s. Between 1768 and 1779, Captain James Cook led three British voyages of exploration probing the Pacific and visiting Australia, New Zealand, and Hawaii.

△ The *Victoria* was the only surviving ship from a fleet of five that set out to circle the globe in 1519. Its return to Spain three years later proved to Europeans that the world was round.

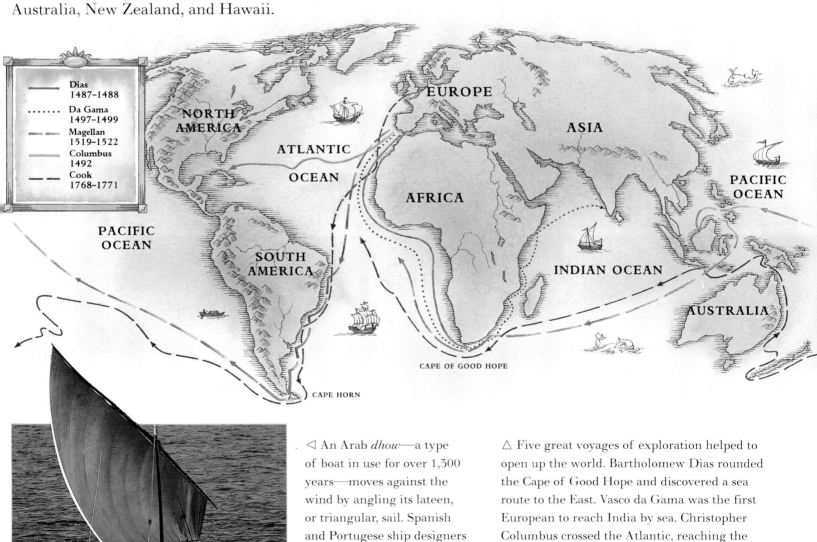

——	Dias 1487–1488
······	Da Gama 1497–1499
— - —	Magellan 1519–1522
——	Columbus 1492
– – –	Cook 1768–1771

NORTH AMERICA

ATLANTIC OCEAN

EUROPE

ASIA

AFRICA

PACIFIC OCEAN

PACIFIC OCEAN

SOUTH AMERICA

INDIAN OCEAN

AUSTRALIA

CAPE OF GOOD HOPE

CAPE HORN

◁ An Arab *dhow*—a type of boat in use for over 1,300 years—moves against the wind by angling its lateen, or triangular, sail. Spanish and Portugese ship designers in the 1400s copied this type of sail to make their vessels faster and more maneuverable.

△ Five great voyages of exploration helped to open up the world. Bartholomew Dias rounded the Cape of Good Hope and discovered a sea route to the East. Vasco da Gama was the first European to reach India by sea. Christopher Columbus crossed the Atlantic, reaching the Americas. Ferdinand Magellan's expedition circled the world, and James Cook's voyages charted the coasts and islands of the Pacific.

Advances in Navigation

Without navigation equipment it is easy to become lost in the open ocean. Most early sailors kept within sight of land, but bolder mariners steered by steady winds or currents, or by following migrating birds. Even so, many lost their way before more accurate navigation aids were invented.

By 1200, the magnetic compass was being used by European sailors to plot direction. Later, the astrolabe and cross staff enabled them to find their latitude (north–south position) by measuring the Sun's midday height or the North Star's height at night.

By the 1500s, latitude could be measured with some accuracy. Longitude (east–west position) remained a problem for another two centuries. Measuring longitude, which relied on precise time-keeping, was finally made possible in the 1760s with the development of accurate clocks called chronometers.

The twentieth century has seen many advances in navigation. Gyroscopic compasses, which are unaffected by magnetic forces, always give exact readings. Loran (long-range navigation) allows a ship to determine its position using radio signals beamed from a pair of transmitters. Radar helps a navigator locate obstructions, while ships' computers receiving signals from satellites can plot positions to within 100 feet (30 m).

△ In the 1500s, navigators used the astrolabe to calculate latitude by observing the Sun at midday.

△ At night, a navigator held a cross staff to his eye and slid the cross piece to line up with the horizon and a star. A scale along the cross staff's arm gave the star's height, enabling the ship's latitude to be measured.

▽ In the late 1500s, the maps of Gerardus Mercator introduced a new way of showing the globe on a flat piece of paper. His system, which used lines of latitude and longitude, helped navigators plot more accurate routes.

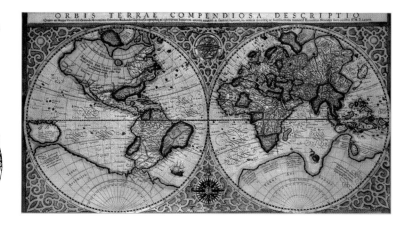

◁ The English naturalist Charles Darwin used this sextant on his voyage around the world betwen 1831 and 1836. Sextants are still used today to determine latitude.

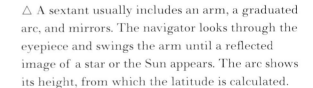

▷ In this Micronesian stick map, curved sticks stand for ocean swells and the shells represent islands. Micronesian seafarers used such maps to chart parts of the Pacific.

△ A sextant usually includes an arm, a graduated arc, and mirrors. The navigator looks through the eyepiece and swings the arm until a reflected image of a star or the Sun appears. The arc shows its height, from which the latitude is calculated.

△ A radar screen helps a navigator to plot a course. Radar bounces radio signals off a target. The returning signals indicate the position of obstructions and other vessels even in thick fog.

▷ Harrison's chronometer of 1760 allowed longitude to be measured by comparing the time in London with the local midday time. This enabled navigators to calculate their east–west position accurately.

Diving Underwater

Until the advent of underwater breathing equipment, only pearl and sponge divers glimpsed what lay more than a few feet below the sea's surface. Exploring and working below the waves only became possible in the early 1800s with the develoment of basic breathing equipment. A person at the surface pumped air through a tube into the diver's helmet below. Weighted down with lead, these divers recovered valuable cargo from sunken ships.

Many of these early divers suffered serious problems. As the diver rose, dissolved air in the blood formed bubbles causing pains called the bends, or even paralysis known as the staggers. Divers who go too deep or stay down too long still face the same risks. Scientists now know that the deeper or longer you dive, the slower you must come up to avoid injury. An invention that helped to solve this problem was JIM, a reinforced diving suit enabling divers to breathe air at atmospheric pressure. However, these divers still have to be tethered by cable.

Scuba divers are much more mobile. Their scuba equipment (Self-Contained Underwater Breathing Apparatus) allows complete freedom of movement while breathing from cylinders strapped to their backs.

△ A JIM suit protects a diver from the crushing water pressure at depths of up to 2,000 feet (600 m). This diving system is named after the first person to wear one.

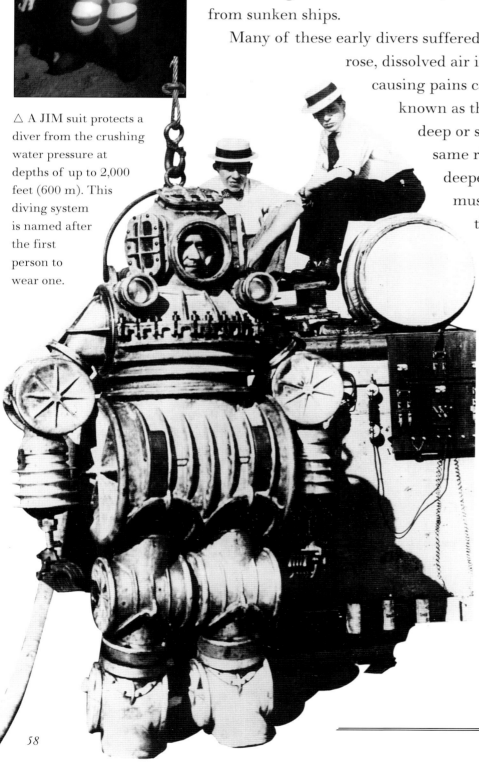

◁ This metal monster, designed in Germany during the 1930s, was an early attempt to create a pressure-proof diving suit. Unlike modern JIM suits, it offered the diver very little flexibility when working underwater.

▷ A commercial diver cuts bolts from a clamp on the legs of an oil production platform. Cleaning, painting, cutting, and welding are among the underwater tasks performed on oil rigs, pipelines, and ships' hulls.

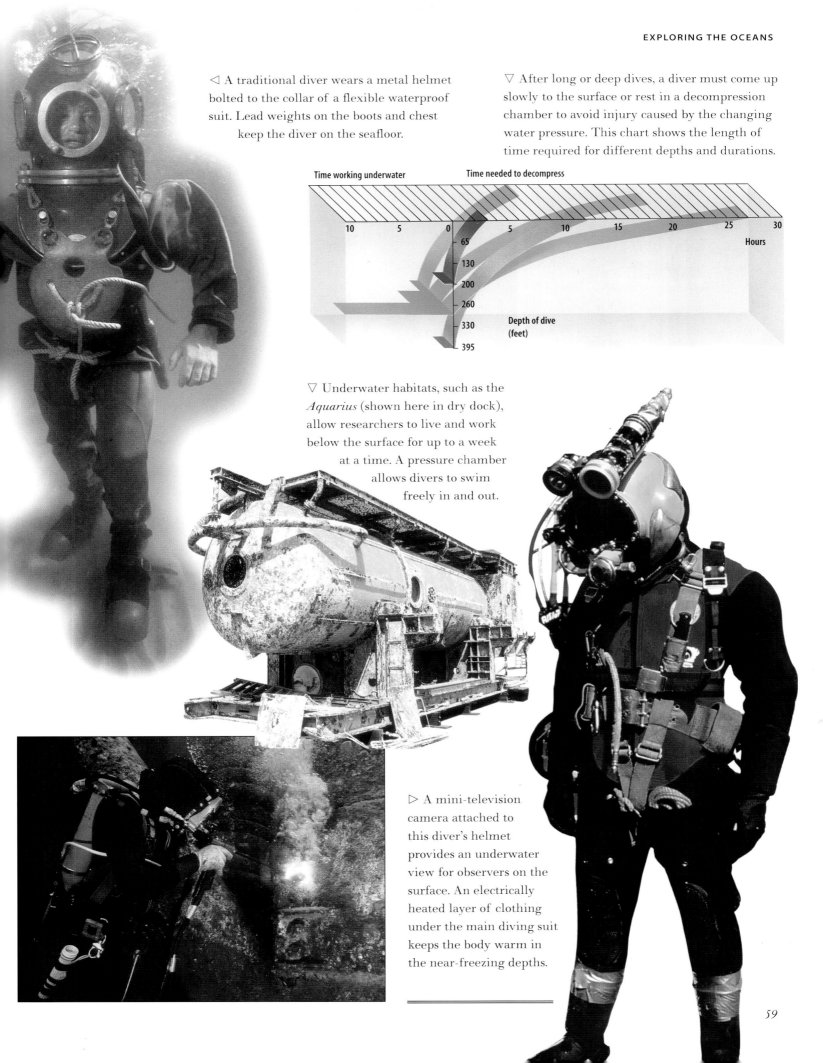

◁ A traditional diver wears a metal helmet bolted to the collar of a flexible waterproof suit. Lead weights on the boots and chest keep the diver on the seafloor.

▽ After long or deep dives, a diver must come up slowly to the surface or rest in a decompression chamber to avoid injury caused by the changing water pressure. This chart shows the length of time required for different depths and durations.

Time working underwater

Time needed to decompress

10   5   0   5   10   15   20   25   30

Hours

65
130
200
260

Depth of dive (feet)

330
395

▽ Underwater habitats, such as the *Aquarius* (shown here in dry dock), allow researchers to live and work below the surface for up to a week at a time. A pressure chamber allows divers to swim freely in and out.

▷ A mini-television camera attached to this diver's helmet provides an underwater view for observers on the surface. An electrically heated layer of clothing under the main diving suit keeps the body warm in the near-freezing depths.

Underwater Discoveries

Until this century, the world below the waves remained almost unexplored. Today however, geological, biological, archaeological, and salvage work is made possible by divers, submersibles and specialized equipment such as underwater television cameras and sonar.

Cameras can film seafloor and mineral deposits in the making. They have recorded molten lava oozing up through cracks in spreading ridges, as well as columns of black, mineral-rich water spewed out by hydrothermal vents, or black smokers, which can also be found there.

Between them, scuba divers and submersibles have taught us much of what we know about sea life. Creatures at every depth have been studied, from the shallow-water fish of coral reefs and polar seas, to the marine life that exists in ocean trenches tens of thousands of feet down.

Scuba-diving archaeologists find, excavate and recover old shipwrecks and their cargoes. Commercial divers and submersibles locate and salvage modern shipwrecks and their contents. Underwater vehicles have even located and recovered items from the liner *Titanic*, lying 12,400 feet (3,780 m) deep on the Atlantic seafloor.

△ A diver uses an air dredge to help uncover an ancient shipwreck. This equipment works like a vacuum cleaner, sucking up loose sediment.

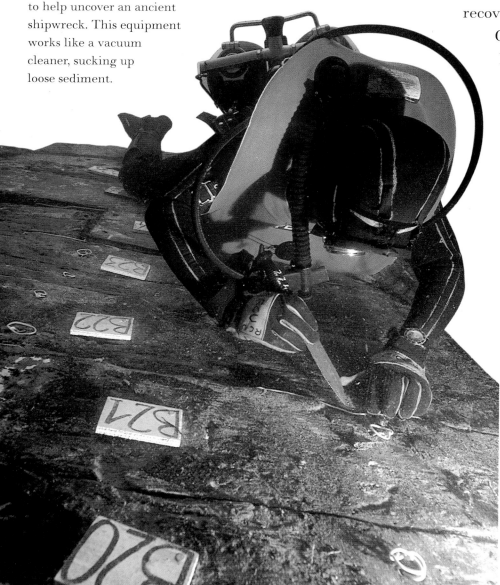

◁ An archaeologist probes the wreck of a Danish merchant vessel. The site is divided into small sections and numbered. The position of each find is recorded on a grid, just as on land. This site lies 230 feet (70 m) deep in the Mediterranean Sea off the French town of Villefranche, where the ship sank over 300 years ago.

◁ Filmed by a submersible's camera, unbroken plates from the *Titanic*'s kitchen lie on the ocean floor more than 80 years after the ship sank. Another view (*right*) shows its foremast lantern and the exploring mechanical arm of the submersible *Nautile*.

◁ The wooden hull of the *Mary Rose* stands in a display hall at Portsmouth dockyard in England. This warship was sunk off the English coast in 1545 and raised in 1982. It is sprayed with chemicals to preserve the remaining wood.

▽ A diver films molten lava seeping from a shallow seabed. At deeper levels, cameras are carried aboard submersibles or towed on special sleds and operated remotely.

◁ A scuba diver, with the submersible *Atlantis* in the background, collects fish samples. Films and samples taken by divers, and submersibles with mechanical arms, have shed new light on the marine creatures that live at different depths.

Sounding the Depths

The modern science of oceanography—the detailed study of the oceans—began more than a century ago. Between 1872 and 1876, scientists on HMS *Challenger* sailed nearly 69,000 miles (111,000 km) measuring temperature and currents, and sampling seawater and sea life. More was learned about the sea than had been discovered during all preceding history.

Since the *Challenger* expedition, scientists' understanding of the oceans has been transformed by a range of specialized devices. Carousel water samplers check salinity and temperature at different levels. Towed bathythermographs record changes in temperature and water pressure. Underwater buoys and swallow floats provide information about currents below the surface.

Corers, dredges, and grab samplers are among the devices used for sampling seabed life and sediment. Deep-sea drilling by research ships such as the *JOIDES Resolution* brings up rock samples from deep below the ocean floor. Seismic profiling can also indicate what lies under the seabed. Sailors once measured ocean depths by lowering cannonballs on piano wire. Today, echo sounders and television cameras let scientists precisely map underwater hills and valleys.

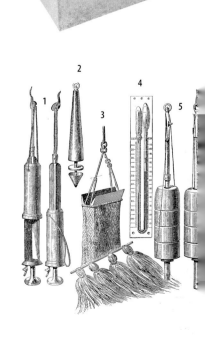

◁ The pioneering expedition of HMS *Challenger* in the 1870s dramatically increased understanding of the oceans. Thousands of measurements were taken, and many species of plants and animals new to science were discovered.

▷ Instruments used by the scientists on the *Challenger* included slip water bottles (1), sounding leads (2), dredges (3), deep-sea thermometers (4), and sounding machines (5).

▽ TOBI (Towed Ocean Bottom Instrument) uses sonar and advanced image-processing methods to record deep-sea features as little as 6 feet (2 m) across. TOBI is lowered by cable and can operate at depths of up to 20,000 feet (6,000 m).

△ A bathyscan, towed underwater by a research vessel, sends out a broad beam of acoustic pulses. This echo sounding system can scan an area of seabed up to 1,650 feet (500 m) across every second. The returning signals are converted into detailed maps of the continental shelf and the seabed.

◁ The research ship *JOIDES Resolution* can drill through more than 6,500 feet (2,000 m) of seafloor in water up to 27,000 feet (8,200 m) deep. Samples taken have revealed spreading seafloor, as well as a drowned plateau in the Indian Ocean.

△ A carousel water sampler is hauled aboard a reseach ship. This device holds 24 sampling bottles that can be operated at different times and depths. Samples are taken to measure water temperature and the chemicals in seawater.

Surveying the Surface

Mapping ocean currents and winds began long before scientists started plumbing the depths. The aim was to save time on sea voyages. In 1769, Benjamin Franklin published a chart of the Gulf Stream. James Rennell's *Currents of the Atlantic Ocean* appeared in 1832. In 1847, Lieutenant Matthew F. Maury of the United States Navy produced a chart of North Atlantic currents and winds based on notes from ships' logs. Sailing ships using such charts cut weeks off long ocean voyages by following favorable currents and winds.

Today, scientists use sophisticated techniques to chart currents.

△ Lieutenant Matthew F. Maury (1806–1873) used information from ships' logs to compile charts on winds and currents in the North Atlantic. In 1855 he published *The Physical Geography of the Sea*. This work covers currents, winds, depths, climates, and storms.

▽ A plankton net is used to take samples of the tiny marine organisms found in surface waters. Nets made from the finest mesh trap phytoplankton, while slightly coarser nets catch the larger zooplankton.

Dyes released into the water identify currents and show up from the air. Buoys that drift with the water can be tracked by satellite. Current meters moored to anchored buoys or hung from ships record the speed and direction of a current in any one place.

To sample surface sea life, research vessels tow long, fine-meshed plankton nets. These show the number and types of plankton in given quantities of seawater.

Oceanographic satellites, orbiting hundreds or thousands of miles above the ocean, allow scientists to observe surface features on a global scale. Satellites such as GEOSAT, ERS-1, and ERS-2 monitor sea level, wave height, wave direction, surface temperatures, wind speeds, currents, sea ice, and levels of marine plant life.

△ A current meter is checked before scientists lower it into the water. This device has a vane that lines up with the current's flow, and a rotor that senses current speed. Inside the protective casing, magnetic tape records this information together with temperature and water pressure.

◁ From high above the Earth, the ERS-1 (European Remote Sensing) satellite keeps track of surface temperature, currents, and other changing features of the ocean's surface. Powered by a solar panel, it operates 24 hours a day. Since the 1970s, remote sensing from satellites has become an increasingly valuable tool for studying the oceans.

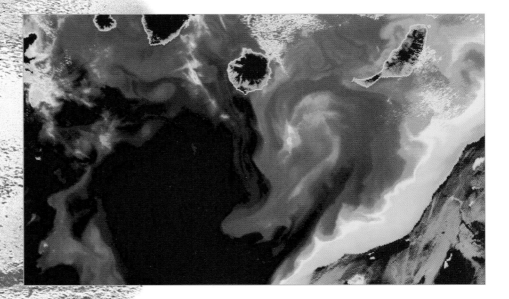

△ This satellite image taken by ERS-1 indicates different surface temperatures in the Atlantic Ocean off northwest Africa (*bottom right*). The warmest parts show up in yellow, the coldest in blue. The large swirling purple area shows a warm eddy, measuring 125 miles (200 km) across, where cold water mixes with warmer mid-Atlantic water.

Sea Mysteries

▽ There have been many supposed sightings of the *Flying Dutchman*. The legend of this ghost ship is probably based on a real vessel that vanished during the 1600s.

△ In 1945, a squadron of five U.S. bombers flew over the Bermuda Triangle on a training flight. The aircraft and crew were never seen again, even though rescue crews searched the area for five days.

△ In 1872, the *Mary Celeste* was found drifting in the Atlantic Ocean, between the Azores and Portugal. The ship was deserted, although the cargo and most of the equipment had been left on board. No one has been able to explain why this seaworthy ship had been abandoned.

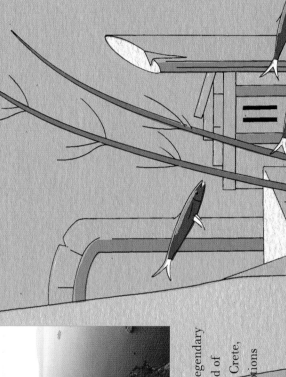

▽ Plato, the ancient Greek philosopher, believed that Atlantis was a rich and powerful civilization, which once flourished on a large island in the Atlantic Ocean. According to Plato, the gods destroyed Atlantis to punish its citizens, and the island

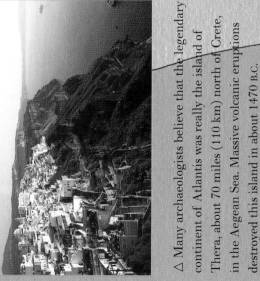

△ Many archaeologists believe that the legendary continent of Atlantis was really the island of Thera, about 70 miles (110 km) north of Crete, in the Aegean Sea. Massive volcanic eruptions destroyed this island in about 1470 B.C.

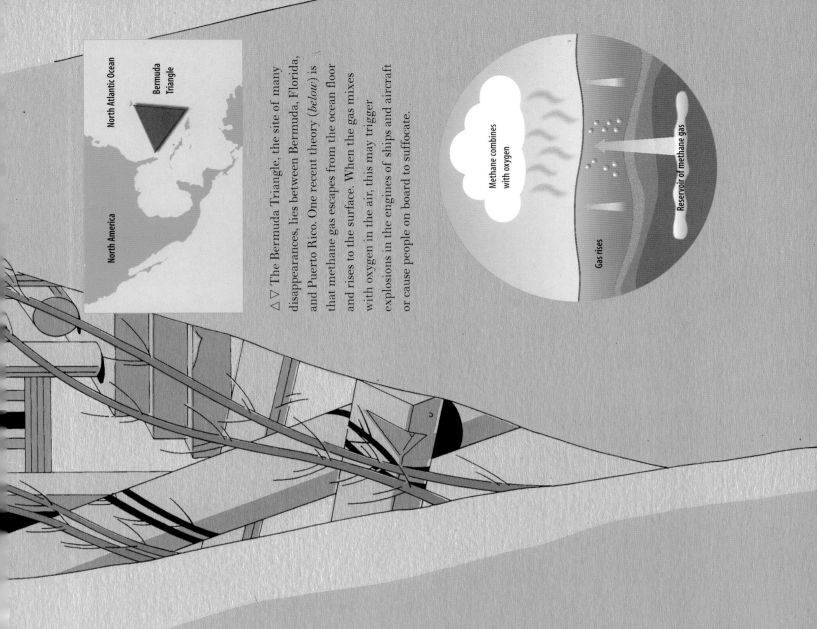

North America

North Atlantic Ocean

Bermuda Triangle

△▽ The Bermuda Triangle, the site of many disappearances, lies between Bermuda, Florida, and Puerto Rico. One recent theory (*below*) is that methane gas escapes from the ocean floor and rises to the surface. When the gas mixes with oxygen in the air, this may trigger explosions in the engines of ships and aircraft or cause people on board to suffocate.

Methane combines with oxygen

Gas rises

Reservoir of methane gas

There are many legends and stories about ships, aircraft, and even entire lands that have vanished without a trace into the oceans.

Several tales tell of countries that sank into the sea. The mythical lost land of Lyonesse off Cornwall in Britain is possibly based on a coast that drowned when melting ice sheets raised sea level worldwide about 10,000 years ago. Ancient Greeks wrote of the vanished civilization of Atlantis. The source for this legend might be the volcanic Aegean island of Thera that erupted in about 1470 B.C. Lemuria was a continent that sank into the Indian Ocean, according to scientists who were trying to explain how the same kinds of land animals once lived on the opposite sides of this ocean. (We now know that continents just drifted apart).

The *Flying Dutchman* is one of the most enduring of sea legends. According to one version of the story, this ship is doomed to roam the oceans for eternity, after the captain defied God. However, supposed sightings of this ghost ship are more likely to have been mirages—far-off ships made to seem closer by tricks of the light. A more recent mystery concerns the disappearance of all ten members of the crew aboard the *Mary Celeste*. This deserted sailing ship was found crossing the Atlantic in 1872.

Many theories have been advanced to explain why ships and aircraft have vanished in the so-called Bermuda Triangle. Explanations that have been put forward range from powerful magnetic fields to exploding gases that have risen from the seabed.

Mythical Sea Beasts

▷ Mermaids, according to popular tales, were fish-tailed women who lured sailors into danger. Accounts of mermaids and similar half-human beings go back over 3,000 years.

▽ The sea serpent appears in many ancient myths and sailors' stories around the world. In Viking legends, storms were said to be caused by the writhing of a giant serpent.

Stories of strange sea beasts feature in the folklore of all seafaring nations. Sailors often reported seeing humanlike sea creatures, sea serpents, and monsters with many tentacles. Superstition, rumor, and fear of the unknown helped fuel mariners' tales, which spread quickly from port to port.

Mythical sea beasts include the Norwegian sea monk and the Chinese sea *bonze*. Both were said to have fins as well as human features. These imaginary beings may have been based on skates or rays—flat-bodied fish with winglike fins and unusual markings on their undersides.

◁ In Norwegian folklore, a giant sea monster called the kraken was said to attack ships and pluck helpless sailors from the deck. Reports of long tentacles suggest that mariners had really seen a giant squid or octopus.

Stories of mermaids—women with the lower body of a fish—appear in Hindu legends as well as many European folktales. In many traditions, mermaids used their beauty and songs to lure sailors to their death. Accounts of these fabled creatures were probably inspired by sightings of sea mammals such as sea cows or seals.

Encounters with real animals are also the likely origin of various terrifying sea monsters. Depictions of the kraken, a formidable sea dragon, resemble a giant squid or octopus. Oarfish, leaping dolphins, or even floating masses of seaweed may explain tales of sea serpents.

▽ In Greek legend, the hydra was a water serpent with many heads. It was eventually killed by Hercules, one of the heroes of Greek mythology.

▽ Since the 1930s, there have been many reported sightings of a strange creature in Loch Ness, Scotland. Despite various scientific investigations and possible photographic evidence, there is still no conclusive proof that the Loch Ness monster exists.

△ Sightings of mermaids may have been inspired by the dugong, a sea mammal related to the manatee. In Indonesia, Southeast Asia, the dugong is treated as a sacred animal. Here, a young female dugong is moved from its grazing ground to a local village.

▷ Sea monks appear in both Western and Eastern folklore. Chinese sailors believed that these half-human creatures raised storms and sank ships.

69

The Sea and the Arts

Over the last 250 years the sea has inspired many composers, writers, and painters. But the sea has not always been a subject in its own right. In paintings of the 1400s and 1500s, for example, it was used as a background for gods and goddesses, or historical events.

From the late 1700s, however, the sea began to loom large in poems, paintings, and music. Some artists saw it as a world of terror and mystery, others as a place of gently changing moods or as a setting for pleasure.

Artists such as William Hodges and J. M. W. Turner painted the sea to show nature at its most powerful. Their pictures show the helplessness of people in the face of an overwhelming sea storm or waterspout. The terrifying dangers of the open sea are brilliantly caught in the shipwreck paintings of Winslow Homer. Mystery and terror also feature in works of literature and music, such as Herman Melville's novel *Moby Dick* and Richard Wagner's opera *The Flying Dutchman*.

The sea's changing moods fascinated French impressionist painters of the late 1800s, as well as composers from Felix Mendelssohn to Benjamin Britten. The opera *Peter Grimes*, written by Britten in 1945, shows the sea raging in a storm, glinting in the sun, and sulking in the fog.

△ Winds that blow across the sea are given human form in this detail from *Birth of Venus* (*see bottom right*).

▽ A boat is dwarfed by the raging sea in *The Breaking Wave off Kanagawa*. This print was made by the great Japanese artist Hokusai (1760–1849).

△ A whale snatches up a boat in a poster for a movie based on *Moby Dick*, the novel by the American writer Herman Melville (1819–1891). This adventure tells the story of Captain Ahab's fanatical hunt to catch a fierce white whale that eventually kills him.

◁ A lone man drifts helplessly on a battered boat circled by sharks. *The Gulf Stream*, by the American artist Winslow Homer (1836–1910), captures human powerlessness when faced by one of the ocean's many dangers.

△ A visit to the Scottish island of Staffa inspired the German composer Felix Mendelssohn (1809–1847) to compose *The Hebrides (Fingal's Cave)*.

▷ The sea provided little more than a background for Renaissance paintings, such as *Birth of Venus*. This picture by the Italian artist Sandro Botticelli (1445–1510) is based on a Greek myth. It tells the story of how Venus—the goddess of love—was born in the sea and blown ashore in a seashell.

△ A sandy beach crowded with bathers features in *The Beach in Front of the Casino Café*, by the American artist Martha Walter (1875–1976). By the mid-1800s railroads had put coasts within easy reach of city-dwellers. Artists began to paint the seaside as a popular playground for vacationers.

Ships and Seaways

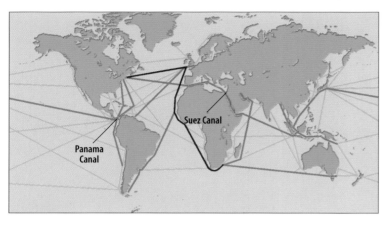

△ This map shows the world's main shipping routes. Darker lines indicate the lanes with the heaviest traffic. The Suez and Panama canals save ships from long journeys around Africa and South America.

Strong steel hulls and propellers turned by powerful turbine engines make modern ships far bigger and faster than the vessels of the past. Huge oil-carrying supertankers include the *Jahre Viking*—nearly one-third of a mile long and weighing more than half a million tons. The container ship *Regina Maersk* holds 6,000 containers, each one a truckload of goods. Car ferries can carry up to 400 vehicles at a time and transport passengers to their destination at speeds of up to 40 knots.

World trade depends on ships plying the invisible sea lanes between continents. Artificial waterways have helped reduce some sea journeys by thousands of miles. The St Lawrence Seaway takes craft into the heart of North America. Large sea-going vessels pass through the Suez and Panama canals—short-cuts between oceans that save up to 7,500 miles (12,000 km).

▷ Large twin-hulled vessels, such as this SeaCat catamaran, carry cars and passengers across short sea crossings.

▽ During the 1991 Persian Gulf War, the 885-foot (270 m) USS *Missouri* was the largest battleship in active service.

△ Fireboats tackle a blazing oil tanker. High-powered pumps draw water from the sea or spray foam over the fire when flammable gases or liquids are involved.

▽ Workers removed 210 million cubic yards of earth and rock from the Gaillard Cut at the eastern end of the Panama Canal.

▽ The Panama Canal links the Atlantic to the Pacific. Constructed between 1907 and 1914, this 50-mile (82 km) waterway allows ships to travel between the two oceans without sailing around South America. A series of locks raises and lowers ships between different water levels.

Great ports cope with a huge volume of traffic that increases each year. By the mid-1990s, Rotterdam was the world's busiest port. Hong Kong and Singapore City each handle more than 12 million containers a year. Radar displays enable Singapore's traffic controllers to let 300 ships in and out of the port every day. New computer-controlled cranes will allow an extra five million containers to be handled each year.

◁ Stacked rows of containers await removal in the port of Singapore City. Traffic controllers, assisted by computers and radar, ensure the smooth running of one of the busiest ports in Southeast Asia. Containers transported by ship hold goods of all kinds. They can be loaded and unloaded quickly by dockside cranes.

◁ The Suez Canal in Egypt cuts across 100 miles (162 km) of desert. Opened in 1869, it links the Mediterranean with the Indian Ocean. Its size has been increased several times to allow for more traffic and larger ships.

Submarines and Submersibles

For over 200 years submarines have been developed and used for military purposes. In 1776, the *Turtle*, powered by a hand crank, launched an unsuccessful attack on a British warship during the American Revolution. By 1900, submarines were being driven by diesel-electric engines. However, the need to recharge batteries and provide oxygen for the crew and engine limits the length of time these submarines can spend underwater.

Nuclear-powered submarines, first introduced in the mid-1950s, do not have these drawbacks. The engines require no air, and the crew breathes oxygen that has been chemically recycled.

Engineers also developed submersibles, or underwater vessels, for peaceful purposes. In 1934, William Beebe watched underwater life from his bathysphere—a steel chamber lowered nearly half a mile into the sea off Bermuda. In 1960, the bathyscaphe *Trieste* dived 6.8 miles (10.9 km) deep in the Pacific. Since then, researchers have probed the depths with highly maneuverable submersibles and remote-controlled vehicles.

△ At 564 feet (172 m) long, the Russia's Typhoon-class submarines are the biggest in the world. Like other nuclear submarines, they can remain underwater indefinitely.

▷ The submersible *Alvin* is capable of diving 13,120 feet (4,000 m). A remotely-operated vehicle, *Jason Junior* (*right*), can be operated with remote controls from within the submersible. It can be sent to places that are too small or too dangerous for access by *Alvin* directly. In 1985, this tethered robot was used to probe the wreck of the *Titanic* in the Atlantic Ocean.

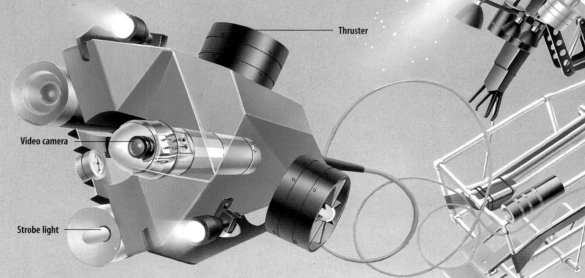

Thruster

Video camera

Strobe light

◁ The *Johnson Sea-Link* submersible can descend to almost 3,280 feet (1,000 m). A pressure chamber allows divers to use it as a base.

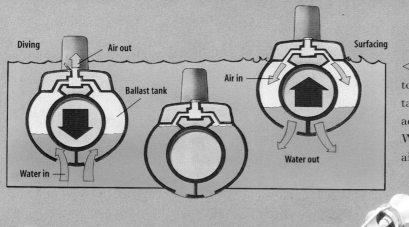

Diving | Air out | Ballast tank | Air in | Surfacing | Water in | Water out

◁ A submarine uses ballast, or extra weight, to dive. When air is let out from the ballast tanks, water rushes in to take its place. The additional weight makes the submarine sink. When the water is forced out by pumping in air, the submarine rises again.

◁ The American submersible *Alvin* has made thousands of successful dives since it was first commissioned in 1964. The small cabin has enough room for a crew of three people. Both *Alvin* and *Jason Junior* are propelled and steered by thrusters.

Thrusters

▽ In 1776, the *Turtle*, designed by an American student, went into action in New York Harbor during the American Revolution. This early submarine was operated by one person. The propellers were turned by a hand crank. However, the *Turtle*'s mission to sink a British warship was not a success. It failed in its attempt to attach a small explosive charge to the hull of the enemy ship.

Batteries

Ballast tank

Titanium cabin helps resist extreme water pressure

Food from the Sea

△ A wood and wire cage, filled with lobsters caught off the coast of Brazil, is raised from the sea. Lobster pots, or traps, are baited with fish or fish offal and lowered to the seabed.

Fish provide much of the world's protein food supply. Every year, about 75 million tons of fish are caught. The richest fishing grounds lie where seawater contains plenty of nutrients for the plankton on which fish depend. Mackerel, pollack, herring and tuna are important pelagic, or surface-living, fish. Popular demersal, or bottom-living, fish include cod, flounder, plaice, haddock, and shellfish such as crabs, lobsters, and shrimp.

Inshore, nets are thrown and traps set by hand to catch fish, crabs, and octopuses. Out at sea, sonar devices help fishing boats track down large shoals, and special nets or hooks catch fish living at different depths. Trawlers hunt demersal species by dragging trawl nets over the seabed. Purse seine nets are pulled shut to trap mid-water species. Pelagic fish are either snared on long curtainlike drift nets hung from buoys, or caught on baited hooks attached to long lines.

Small craft may supply one big factory ship, where fish are gutted, frozen, and stored for several weeks. A factory trawler may catch and process up to 600 tons a day. However, intensive fishing can also threaten ocean resources. Overfishing has dramatically reduced the stocks of some species.

▷ The plaice is a species of bottom-dwelling flatfish. It is of great commercial value for the European fishing industry. Trawlers catch plaice in nets dragged along the seabed.

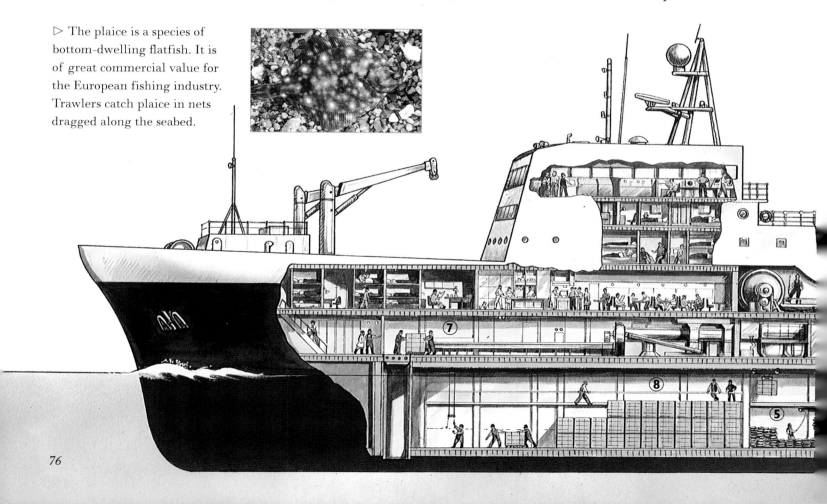

△ Workers cultivate a crop of oysters maturing in shallow seawater off New South Wales, Australia. Oysters are farmed for food and pearl production. The oysters are cultivated on trays or sticks. Other marine organisms grown and farmed around the world include mussels, clams, and seaweed.

▽ A modern factory freezer ship processes fish products at sea. Reeled aboard from the stern, the 2,600-foot (800 m) long net (1) spills the catch into a fish bin (2). The fish are then gutted and cleaned (3). Nothing is wasted. Offal is turned into fish meal (4) and bagged (5). Filleted fish are compressed into blocks of seafood paste (6), then rapidly frozen and packaged (7). The boxes are stored in the refrigerated hold (8). In one day, a modern factory ship can process more than 600 tons of fish.

△ Spanish fishermen in open boats cast a net around a shoal of tuna. As the net closes in on them, the fish are pulled out with hooks.

Mineral Resources

Seawater and the seafloor are rich in minerals and other useful substances. People have extracted salt from seawater for thousands of years. In hot countries, saltwater is pumped into shallow pools and allowed to evaporate. The salt left behind can then be collected. In cold climates, workers separate salt by boiling seawater. Other processes extract most of the world's supply of bromine and magnesium—elements with important industrial uses—from seawater.

Offshore seabeds are a source of building materials such as shells for making cement, and sand and gravel, which are sucked up by powerful pumps into barges. Off the shores of Malaysia and Thailand, engineers quarry sediment for tin-rich cassiterite. Millions of metallic lumps, called manganese nodules, cover parts of the deep ocean floor and may become a useful resource when land-based mines run dry.

Much of the world's oil and gas supply is now piped up from under the floors of shallow seas fringing the continents. Semi-submersible platforms, floating in water 1,000 feet (300 m) deep, can test-drill through 29,500 feet (9,000 m) of seabed rock. Steel or concrete production platforms weighing up to 30,000 tons stand in up to 3,000 feet (900 m) of water.

△ Vast local deposits of iron ore have helped make Detroit, Michigan, one of the world's most important centers for car manufacturing. The ore was formed under an ancient sea that is now part of the North American continent.

◁ A desalination plant in Bahrain separates salt and seawater to produce much-needed freshwater. Bahrain is situated on the Arabian Peninsula where more than half the world's 4,000 desalination plants are found.

△ A dredger scoops up sand from deposits in North Carolina. Worldwide, off-shore dredging produces about 1.2 billion tons of sand and gravel a year. Their main use is in the manufacture of concrete.

▷ Workers in Sri Lanka rake up crusts of salt that have formed in salt pans. The salt is left behind when the hot, tropical sun evaporates the seawater that fills the shallow pools.

▽ Lit up like a city at night, an immense North Sea oil production platform nears completion. After being towed into position, massive stilts resting on the seabed will hold it securely in place above the wildest storm waves.

SEA HAZARDS

The Unstable Surface

S ome of the most treacherous weather events on Earth occur or start out at sea. Warm tropical seas create fierce, circular storms called hurricanes, typhoons, or cyclones. These winds spin at up to 105 mph (170 km/hr) around a calm center. Once over land, a hurricane becomes cut off from the warm water that fuels it, and loses power. However, before this happens, vicious winds and huge waves can overwhelm ships and devastate coasts.

In 1988, Hurricane Gilbert struck the Caribbean and Mexico causing about 300 deaths and millions of dollars worth of damage. These storms can also drive the sea inland, drowning low-lying land. Cyclones in southern Asia cause frequent flooding and huge loss of life.

Devastating waves can also be set off by earthquakes under the sea. Knowns as tsunamis, these waves are as fast as a jet aircraft and can rear close to 100 feet (30 m) high on entering a bay. Many of the estimated 60,000 people who died during the Lisbon earthquake of 1755 were drowned when a tsunami struck this Portugese city at the same time.

Waterspouts are twisting columns of air that suck up water from the sea's surface. Although they pose a hazard to small craft, they are usually more spectacular than dangerous.

◁ Storm waves sweep inshore as Hurricane Andrew hits Florida in August 1992.

▷ A waterspout is a tornado that forms over water, usually in warm, tropical seas. A spinning column of air drops from a cloud and sucks up water. Waterspouts rarely cause major damage.

◁△ This satellite picture (*left*) shows Typhoon Violet over the Philippines in 1996. The swirling bed of clouds extends hundreds of miles outward from the central eye. When this kind of storm reaches land the winds can tear houses apart, fell trees, and toss boats ashore (*above*).

▽ Cyclones often cause floods in Bangladesh in southern Asia. In 1970, a storm surge in the Bay of Bengal drowned huge areas of low-lying land. Some estimates say that a million people lost their lives.

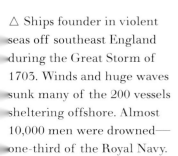

△ Ships founder in violent seas off southeast England during the Great Storm of 1703. Winds and huge waves sunk many of the 200 vessels sheltering offshore. Almost 10,000 men were drowned— one-third of the Royal Navy.

Hidden Dangers

Ships face many dangers at sea. Icebergs that have drifted from polar regions into shipping lanes are one of the most feared of all naturally-occurring hazards. In 1912, just over 1,500 people drowned when the liner *Titanic* hit an iceberg. After this disaster, ice patrols began to keep watch for dangerous, drifting icebergs in the North Atlantic.

Underwater rocks and reefs have also been a risk since ships first put to sea. Shifting sandbanks are another invisible menace. Since 1500, more than 5,000 ships have foundered on the Goodwin Sands off southeast England. In recent years, several supertankers have run aground off Alaska, France, and England.

Disasters have also been caused by human errors such as faulty ship design, overloading, navigational mistakes, and even the failure to close a car ferry's sea doors. Poor maintenance killed 167 people in 1988 when a fire at sea gutted the *Piper Alpha* platform, a North Sea oil rig. However, the greatest of all sea catastrophes occured during World War II when a Soviet submarine sank the German liner *Wilhelm Gustloff* and 7,700 passengers lost their lives.

△ Even in clear weather, icebergs can be a danger to ships that sail too close— 88 percent of a castle iceberg lurks invisibly under the sea.

▽ An aerial photograph shows salvage work on the wrecked and still smoking *Piper Alpha* oil platform. The explosion, in 1988, sparked off by a gas leak, caused the North Sea's worst-ever oil rig disaster.

TITANIC DISASTER GREAT LOSS OF LIFE

EVENING NEWS

◁ In 1912, newspaper headlines around the world reported the sinking of the ocean liner *Titanic*. On her maiden voyage from England to New York City, the world's largest ship struck an iceberg in the freezing waters of the North Atlantic. Believed to be unsinkable, the double-hulled liner sank in about two and a half hours with the loss of over 1,500 lives.

△ In 1993, the tanker *Braer* leaked oil and sank after grounding on rocks off the Shetland Islands. Even worse oil spills have occurred when supertankers have snagged on hidden reefs.

▷ Modern-day pirates in fast, small boats pose a major threat to cargo ships sailing off Indonesia. Crews fend them off with barbed wire fencing and jets of water squirted from hoses.

Seas at Risk

More than ever before, oceans are threatened by people. A number of coasts are particularly at risk. Tropical coral reefs are poisoned by pollution and torn up for building materials. Tropical mangrove forests are felled for their wood or to make space for shrimp farms. Elsewhere, contractors build marinas where salt marshes once stood.

Pollution has badly affected the shores and inshore waters of closed-in seas such as the Baltic and Mediterranean. City sewage, chemical waste from factories, and fertilizers and pesticides from farms escape into rivers that flow into the sea. In open waters, ships spill oil and drop garbage overboard.

Marine life is under threat from all kinds of pollution and people's behavior. For example, millions of seabirds, fish, and turtles are killed each year by plastic products. Overfishing has also had a devastating effect with some species in danger of extinction. In the Pacific, the use of poison and dynamite to catch fish has wiped out entire coral communities.

△ In 1982, an invasion of comb jellies severely depleted fish stocks in the Black Sea. The comb jellies had been accidentally brought over in the ballast water of a visiting ship from the United States. Lacking natural enemies, they rapidly multiplied and destroyed vast numbers of fish eggs, fish fry, and plankton.

▽▷ Burning oil fires polluted land and sea when the retreating Iraqi army destroyed Kuwaiti oil wells during the Persian Gulf War, in 1991. In the Gulf, thousands of seabirds and other marine creatures died as a result of the spills.

◁ A vacationer rows through the heavily polluted waters of the Adriatic. Waste products from cities and factories have made this part of the Mediterranean one of the world's most polluted seas.

◁ A shark lies tangled up in a gill net. Seals, dolphins, and albatrosses are also frequent victims, caught accidentally in nets and hooks on long lines.

▽ Parts of a coral reef that once supported thousands of creatures were destroyed to provide building materials for this home in Colombia.

▽ Fences called groins are designed to protect beaches from coastal erosion. However, groins can also cause erosion by depriving beaches of the sand and gravel that buffer them against the sea's attack.

Saving Seas and Coasts

Many governments are now aware of the need to protect coasts and offshore waters from pollution and damage.

First aid for oil spills includes oil-dispersing chemicals and floating booms that help to stop oil spreading into narrow bays. But the only truly effective action is to stop pollution occurring in the first place. In 1976, Mediterranean countries agreed on an action plan to prevent sewage and chemicals from flowing into the Mediterranean. Asian countries have begun to conserve mangrove forests, and over 60 nations now protect coral reefs.

Engineers are also discovering improved ways of saving coasts from erosion. In some places, they have found that soft sea defenses (artificial beaches) are better than hard ones (concrete walls) at protecting shores from wave erosion.

Nations have begun to enforce laws to prevent the overfishing of wild species. Many governments now discourage the netting of unwanted wild species and have created protected areas. By the mid-1990s, 1,200 marine protected areas existed worldwide. However, there is still much to be done.

△ A floating boom tried to stop oil spreading through Prince William Sound, Alaska, after the supertanker *Exxon Valdez* ran aground in 1989. The spill of 10 million gallons was one of the world's worst pollution incidents. By 1992, the area was beginning to recover.

◁ A tidal barrier forms part of a system of sea defenses protecting the low-lying Netherlands against fierce North Sea storms. Sluice gates are an added safeguard to prevent floods swamping Europe's largest port, Rotterdam.

◁ A team of ecologists have to race against time to clear up a major oil spill. They use scrapers, booms, and pumps to remove oil from a Welsh beach. This spillage came from the tanker *Sea Empress*, which struck rocks offshore early in 1996. A year later, the surface of the beach was clean and local wildlife had virtually recovered as a result of hard work, winds, and waves.

◁ Waves along the Florida coast were gradually eating into the shore, threatening to wash away Miami's waterside hotels (*left*). Vacationers can now safely enjoy 15 miles (25 km) of artificial beach created from imported sand. By preventing erosion, this beach restoration project helps to keep the sea at bay.

▽ Fishery protection officers stop trawlers from other countries overfishing their waters. This Canadian officer is making a careful inspection of a Spanish trawler's catch. In British waters, a police boat (*right*) escorts a foreign trawler arrested for illegal fishing.

Future Prospects

People will always depend on the sea's many resources. As wild fish stocks decline, more people are turning to fish farming. The billions of shrimplike crustaceans called krill also offer a potential food supply, and small-scale harvesting has already begun.

The seabed holds vast mineral deposits. Deep-sea trawling for manganese nodules, the extraction of methane gas and the mining of spreading ridges for copper and zinc will become increasingly important as resources on land dwindle. However, high costs make deep-sea mining unlikely until well into the twenty-first century.

Scientists are learning more about the crucial part that oceans play in the Earth's climate. If global warming continues, people will have to cope with melting ice sheets that raise ocean levels worldwide, drowning atolls and low-lying coasts. Planting mangroves could protect tropical deltas better than building high seawalls, but large tracts of low coast would have to be abandoned. Climatic change could also "switch off" the North Atlantic Drift that warms western Europe. If that happens, London might become as cold as the icy Labrador coast in the North Atlantic.

One way or another, the future of the Earth and its inhabitants is closely bound up with the oceans.

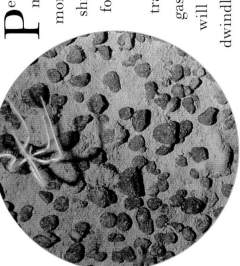

△ Billions of manganese nodules litter the seabed. These metallic lumps are rich in manganese, iron, copper, nickel, and cobalt. However, until less expensive ways are found to mine them, manganese nodules remain a vast, untapped resource.

▽ The oceans would rise some 200 feet (60 m) and drown cities if the ice caps suddenly melted. Some scientists believe that an increase of about 12 inches (30 cm) by the year 2050 is more likely, as a result of global warming. Even so, this would cause severe flooding in low-lying areas.

△ Billions of krill live in the oceans and provide the main source of food for baleen whales. Harvesting krill for human consumption has already begun. As well as being rich in protein, they contain chitin, a substance of great value for the medical industry.

△ If certain ocean currents are disrupted by changes in climate, London could one day have winters as cold and icy as this one in Labrador, Canada. Although on the same latitude as Labrador, the British Isles are kept warm by the North Atlantic Drift.

Oceanographers

Many people have contributed to our understanding of the oceans since the 1700s.

Alexander Agassiz (1835–1910)

Swiss-American marine scientist and engineer. He used his engineering skills to develop new techniques for taking samples and soundings. Agassiz believed, incorrectly, that no marine life existed beyond shallow depths in the sea. Between 1877 and 1880, he studied plankton levels in the Pacific and Atlantic.

Robert Ballard (b. 1942)

American oceanographer who has made over 50 voyages in submersibles. In 1977, Ballard and John Corliss discovered hydrothermal vents 8,200 feet (2,500 m) deep in the Pacific Ocean. He has also explored many shipwrecks, such as the German battleship *Bismark* and the ocean liner *Titanic*.

William Beebe (1877–1962)

American naturalist and explorer who, in 1934, made a record-breaking dive of 3,027 feet (923 m) in a bathysphere.

John Buchanan (1844–1925)

British oceanographer who devised a stop-cock water bottle for sampling, used during the *Challenger* voyage (1872–1876). He later demonstrated that vertical currents carry cold water to the surface. Buchanan also produced one of the first reliable surface temperature maps of the oceans.

Gustave-Gaspard Coriolis (1792–1843)

French scientist who described the "Coriolis effect." This is the force that results from the Earth's rotation and deflects winds and ocean currents moving north or south.

Jacques Yves Cousteau (b. 1910)

French undersea explorer who helped invent the aqualung diving apparatus in 1943, assisted Jacques Piccard in developing the bathyscaphe, and pioneered underwater color photography. Cousteau has led many expeditions, filming and photographing underwater life worldwide.

Charles Darwin (1809–1882)

British naturalist who developed the theory of evolution by natural selection. He made extensive studies of land and sea organisms during a voyage around the world on HMS *Beagle* (1831–1836). He also produced a still-accepted theory of how atolls form.

Sir George Deacon (1906–1984)

British oceanographer who had a major influence on the development of marine science in Britain. He did important work in Antarctic waters and developed new ways of measuring deep ocean currents and analyzing waves.

Robert Dietz (1914–1995)

American oceanographer who discovered that new rock wells up at oceanic ridges. In 1960, he proposed that spreading seafloor formed ocean basins.

Anton Dohrn (1840–1909)

German zoologist who worked with Ernst Haeckel. Dohrn was the founder of the world's first marine biological research station, opened in Naples, Italy, in 1873.

Vagn Walfrid Ekman (1874–1954)

Swedish oceanographer who made important discoveries about the relationship between ocean currents, surface winds, and different layers of water. He also invented the Ekman meter to measure the speed and direction of currents.

Maurice Ewing (1906–1974)

American marine geologist who showed that oceanic crust is much thinner than continental crust. In 1957, he discovered the deep central rift in the Mid-Atlantic Ridge. His work supported the seafloor spreading theory of Harry Hess.

Edward Forbes (1815–1854)

British naturalist who studied marine life and believed that algae was found only near the surface. He also produced important studies on mollusks and echinoderms.

Johann Forschammer (1794–1865)

Danish chemist and geologist who determined the major components of seawater.

Ernst Haeckel (1834–1919)

German zoologist who was strongly influenced by Charles Darwin's theories of evolution. Haeckel wrote a number of studies on marine organisms. He coined the terms *nekton* and *benthos*, respectively for swimming and bottom-dwelling marine organisms.

Bruce Heezen (1924–1977)

American oceanographer who pioneered the mapping of the seafloor with echo-sounding equipment. He recognized that a system of submarine ridges with central rift valleys runs through the oceans. With fellow oceanographers Marie Tharp and Maurice Ewing, he produced maps of the Atlantic, Indian, and Pacific seafloors.

Victor Hensen (1835–1924)

German scientist who worked out the quantity of the tiny organisms called plankton living in the oceans.

Harry Hess (1906–1969)

American geologist who helped pioneer the theory of seafloor spreading. While serving with the U.S. Naval Reserve in 1941, Hess also discovered the flat-topped underwater peaks called guyots. Hess Guyot and Hess Deep (an ocean basin) in the Pacific are named after him.

Columbus Iselin (1904–1971)

American oceanographer and captain of the research ship *Atlantis*. He carried out important surveys of the Gulf Stream and North Atlantic during the 1930s.

Lord Kelvin
(1824–1907)
British scientist who devised a tide-predicting machine and improved ships' compasses. In 1857, he was appointed chief consultant on the laying of the first underwater transatlantic telegraph cable.

Martin Knudsen
(1871–1949)
Danish scientist who developed an effective way of measuring salinity—the dissolved salts in water.

Philip Kuenen
(1902–1976)
Dutch geologist who studied ocean basins and coral atolls. Kuenen also showed how currents formed submarine canyons—the deep valleys scarring the continental slope.

Matthew F. Maury
(1806–1873)
American naval officer who wrote the first textbook on oceanography. *The Physical Geography of the Sea* was published in 1855. He also compiled charts of ocean winds and currents that helped to shorten voyages.

Johannes Müller
(1801–1858)
German scientist who made important microscopic studies of marine organisms such as plankton.

John Murray
(1841–1914)
British-Canadian biologist who worked on the *Challenger* expedition (1872–1876) under Charles Wyville Thomson. Murray edited most of the 50 volumes of work resulting from this voyage. He produced a study on coral reefs in 1880.

Fridtjof Nansen
(1861–1930)
Norwegian explorer and oceanographer who studied the drift of Arctic sea ice by deliberately allowing his ship to become frozen in the ice, between 1893 and 1895. He devised Nansen bottles, which sample deep water, and also explained how wind-driven sea currents work.

Jacques Piccard
(b. 1922)
Swiss undersea explorer who made the deepest-ever manned dive, with Don Walsh of the U.S. Navy, in 1960. They descended almost 36,080 feet (11,000 m) into the Mariana Trench in the Pacific Ocean using the bathyscaphe *Trieste*.

James Rennell
(1742–1830)
British geographer who pioneered statistical studies of ocean currents and believed that surface currents were produced by winds.

Roger Revelle
(1909–1991)
American oceanographer who led surveys studying seabed sediment, submarine mountains, and trenches.

Francis Shepard
(1897–1985)
American marine geologist who studied the seafloor and its sediment.

Henry Stommel
(1920–1992)
American oceanographer who made important studies of the Gulf Stream. He was one of the first scientists to investigate ocean circulation at great depths. In 1977, Stommel devised a new way to measure the speeds of ocean currents.

Harald Sverdrup
(1888–1957)
Norwegian oceanographer who carried out important research on wave heights, tides, and currents. Sverdrup took part in a submarine expedition to the North Pole before moving to California in 1935. His work proved of great use to the U.S. Navy during World War II. The Sverdrup Islands in Arctic Canada are named after him.

John Swallow
(b. 1923)
British oceanographer who developed a method of measuring deep ocean currents using special floats that sink to controlled depths. The floats drift freely and can be monitored by a surface ship.

Sir Charles Wyville Thomson (1830–1882)
British oceanographer who led HMS *Challenger*'s four-year expedition (1872–1876) around the world. This voyage helped pioneer modern oceanography. His *Depths of the Sea* (1877) is a major early textbook.

John Wilson Tuzo
(1908–1993)
Canadian geophysicist who studied seafloor spreading and helped to prove the theory of continental drift, originally proposed by Alfred Wegener.

Felix Meinesz Vening
(1887–1966)
Dutch scientist who used a gravity-measuring pendulum device to reveal information about the Earth's crust below the seabed. Vening's work supported later theories on plate tectonics.

Fred Vine
(1939–1988)
British geologist who predicted, with Drummond Matthews, that there should be strips of normally and reversely magnetized crust on either side of mid-ocean ridges. This theory, put forward in 1963, supported seafloor spreading. By 1966, enough evidence had been collected to prove this theory.

Alexander von Humboldt
(1769–1859)
German explorer and scientist who suggested in 1812 that cold deep-water currents flowed toward the Equator from the polar regions.

Emil von Lenz
(1804–1865)
German physicist who claimed that cold water from the far north and south must well up below the Equator to replace warm surface water flowing between the Poles.

Alfred Wegener
(1880–1930)
German scientist who claimed that the continents may once have been linked as one supercontinent that later broke up and drifted on the Earth's surface. This controversial theory, first published in 1915, did not begin to gain acceptance until the 1960s.

Glossary

Abyssal plain The flat floor of an ocean **basin** below a **continental slope**. Its surface consists of a layer of **sediment** covering uneven rock.

Algae Plantlike, single-celled and many-celled organisms with chlorophyll but no true leaves, stems, or roots.

Antarctic Region south of the Antarctic Circle, or simply the cold region around the South Pole—Antarctica and surrounding far southern parts of the Atlantic, Indian, and Pacific oceans.

Arctic Region north of the Arctic Circle, or simply the cold region around the North Pole. It includes the Arctic Ocean and surrounding far northern parts of Europe, Asia, and North America.

Atoll A ring-shaped coral reef surrounded by open sea and enclosing an area of shallow, sheltered water called a lagoon. Atolls grow on the rims of volcanic islands.

Barrier reef A broad coral reef lying parallel to a shore, beyond a wide, deep strip of water. Australia's Great Barrier Reef is the world's longest barrier reef.

Basin A depression in the Earth's surface containing an ocean. It also refers to the part of the ocean floor more than 6,560 feet (2,000 m) below sea level.

Bathyscaphe A deep-diving underwater vessel, comprising a pressure-proof chamber hung below a hollow, buoyant, gasoline-filled float.

Bathysphere A manned, hollow steel sphere lowered by cable into the sea.

Beach Loose material such as rocks, stones, sand grains, or particles of mud lying on a shore between the levels reached by the highest storm waves and lowest low **tides**.

Bends Sickness caused by gas bubbles forming in the bodies of divers rising too quickly.

Bivalves Soft-bodied animals living in a pair of hinged shells which they can open and close. Bivalves include clams, mussels, and oysters.

Bony fish A fish with a bony skeleton. Bony species, such as herring and tuna, outnumber **cartilaginous** (gristly) species, such as sharks and rays, by more than thirty to one.

Buoy A floating object moored to the seabed. Buoys are used as **navigation** aids.

Cartilaginous fish A fish with a cartilaginous, or gristly, skeleton. Cartilaginous fish include sharks and rays. Unlike **bony** fish, they lack a swim bladder—if they stop swimming they sink.

Continental crust The Earth's crust forming the continents.

Continental rise A gentle slope formed by **sediment** at the foot of a **continental slope**.

Continental shelf The rim of a continental landmass. It slopes gently down to about 590 feet (180 m) and ends at the **continental slope**.

Continental slope The rim of a **continental shelf**. It forms a fairly steep slope descending at least 10,000 feet (3,000 m).

Convergent boundary In **plate tectonics**, a place where two of the plates forming the Earth's crust are colliding.

Copepod A tiny, shrimplike creature forming part of the **zooplankton**.

Crustacean A jointed-legged **invertebrate** such as a crab, lobster, or shrimp. Crustaceans have a tough, jointed outer skeleton and breathe through gills.

Current An ocean current is water flowing through the sea. Winds drive surface currents. Deep-sea currents occur where dense water sinks and spreads over the seabed.

Decompression The reduction of pressure on a diver returning to the surface. Controlled decompression (timed rests at different depths or in a decompression chamber) prevents divers from getting the **bends**.

Divergent boundary In **plate tectonics**, a place where two of the plates forming the Earth's crust are moving away from each other.

Echinoderm A spiny-skinned marine **invertebrate** such as a sea urchin, starfish, or sea cucumber.

Estuary The tidal mouth of a river, especially a drowned lowland valley, with mud flats and creeks.

Fjord A deep, steep-sided sea inlet invading a mountain valley, especially one widened and deepened by a glacier.

Food chain The various kinds of plants and animals forming links in a chain of **predators** and prey. A food chain includes **algae** or plants, plant-eating animals, and carnivorous animals.

Fringing reef A reef joined to the shore of an island or continent, with no water between them.

Groin A fence or wall running down a beach at right angles to the shore. Groins help to stop **longshore drift** robbing beaches of sand and shingle.

Guyot A flat-topped seamount.

Gyre A great loop formed by surface **currents** circling in the ocean north or south of the Equator.

Hurricane A tropical Atlantic storm with winds up to 100 mph (170 km/hr). The Pacific Ocean's typhoons and the Indian Ocean's cyclones are similar storms.

Iceberg A mass of ice broken off a land-based glacier or ice sheet and floating in the sea. Most icebergs come from Antarctica and Greenland.

Invertebrate An animal without vertebrae—the bones forming a backbone. Animals with a backbone are known as vertebrates.

Knot A unit used to measure speed at sea. One knot (one nautical mile per hour) equals 1.67 feet (0.51 m) per second.

Krill Small, shrimplike **crustaceans**. Krill teem in **polar** seas, where they form much of the food consumed by various baleen whales.

Longshore drift The movement of sand and shingle along a beach by waves that break on the shore at an angle. The direction of drift depends on the prevailing wind direction.

Magma Molten rock under the Earth's surface. Magma cooling underground forms igneous rocks. Magma that escapes through cracks in the Earth's surface forms lava.

Migration Round trips made by animals seeking breeding grounds or food. Many make these journeys each year, but salmon and certain eels only return once in their lifetime.

Mineral Any of the main ingredients of rocks. These natural substances have atoms that form crystals. Mined natural substances, such as coal and oil, are also often known as minerals.

Mollusk A soft-bodied **invertebrate**, usually with one or two shells. Mollusks include gastropods, such as sea slugs and whelks, cephalopods, such as squids and octopuses, and **bivalves**, such as mussels and oysters.

Navigation Working out the position and direction of a ship or other vehicle.

Neap tide A **tide** when the difference between high and low water is smallest.

Nekton The name for all animals that swim in the sea.

Ocean The salt water covering two-thirds of the Earth, or one of its four major divisions—the Atlantic Ocean, Indian Ocean, Pacific Ocean, or Arctic Ocean.

Oceanography The scientific study of the oceans. This includes the chemicals in seawater, water temperature and pressure, **currents** and waves, and life in the sea.

Ooze Soft, wet mud on the deep ocean floor. The contents of deep-sea oozes include dust and the remains of billions of tiny planktonic organisms.

Phytoplankton Microscopic one-celled **algae** that drift in the surface waters. Like true plants, they produce food from chemicals by using the energy in sunlight.

Plankton The various tiny organisms that drift in the sea's surface waters. Plankton provides the food that most marine creatures depend on, directly or indirectly. See also **phytoplankton** and **zooplankton**.

Plate tectonics Study of the development, movement, and destruction of the so-called lithospheric plates. These carry oceanic and **continental crust** and form the Earth's rigid outer shell.

Polar Relating to the world's far north or far south—the regions around the North Pole or South Pole.

Polyp A sea anemone, coral, or other form of coelenterate. These organisms have a stalk-like body fixed at one end to a rock or other underwater object. The other end has a mouth surrounded by a ring of tentacles.

Predator An animal that preys on others.

Ria A narrow inlet of the sea produced by a rise in sea level or sinking of the land.

Ridge A long, narrow, raised, steep-sided area of the Earth's crust. Spreading ridges on the ocean floor are formed where the Earth's plates diverge.

Rift valley A valley formed where a mass of rock slid down between two plates that were moving apart. A rift valley runs along the crest of a mid-ocean **ridge**.

Salinity The amount of dissolved salts in seawater.

Scuba Short for Self-Contained Underwater Breathing Apparatus. Scuba divers carry their own air supply with them, which lets them swim about freely.

Sea A word used to mean either the ocean or a named part of a particular ocean, for example the Caribbean Sea, a part of the Atlantic Ocean.

Seafloor spreading The process by which lithospheric plates move apart from mid-ocean **ridges**, where new sea-floor is made.

Sea ice Ice formed from frozen seawater.

Seamount A submarine volcanic peak with a summit 3,280 feet (1,000 m) or more above the seafloor.

Sediment Loose particles deposited by water or wind. Inshore sediment includes gravel and boulders. Deep-sea sediment is mainly made up of fine clays.

Sonar Short for SOund Navigation And Ranging. This system locates the position of objects on the surface or underwater by emitting sounds and timing the echoes that bounce back.

Spring tide A **tide** when the difference between high and low water is greatest.

Submarine canyon A deep, narrow, steep-sided valley cut into a **continental slope** by the sudden slide of a mixture of water and **sediment**.

Submersible A manned or remotely operated submarine designed for research in very deep water.

Thermohaline Temperature and **salinity** as they affect the vertical circulation of seawater.

Tide The regular rise and fall of sea level caused by the gravitational pulls of the Moon and Sun on the Earth.

Transform fault A crack in the seafloor cutting across a mid-ocean **ridge** at right angles.

Trench A deep, narrow, steep-sided trough in the ocean floor.

Tsunami A seismic sea wave, set off by a volcanic eruption or submarine earthquake. This low wave rises on reaching shallow water, and can cause considerable damage.

Upwelling The rising of nutrient-rich seawater from deep parts of the sea to the surface.

Water cycle The continual flow of the Earth's water. Water vapor from the sea and land rises into the atmosphere, becoming rain, hail, or snow. These fall on the sea or fill rivers flowing to the sea.

Zooplankton The animals forming part of the **plankton**. Most are tiny and live deep down by day, but rise at night to feed upon **phytoplankton**.

Index

Acknowledgments

The publishers would like to thank the following illustrators for their contributions to this book:

Debbie Cook 22–23, 26*tl*, 28–29, 50–51, 66–67, 68–69; **Peter Dennis** 10*cr*; **Anthony Duke** 8*b*, 11*tr*, 15*t*, 17*br*, 22*bl*, 23*br*, 42–43, 67*r* & *br*, 72*tl*; **Bernard Gudynas** icons, 88–89 (composite) **Ron Hayward** 51*cr*; **Gary Hinks** 8–9, 12–13, 13*br*, 14–15, 16*bl*, 17*tr*, 24*b*, 25*bl* & *br*, 27*c* & *tr*, 52*bl* & *cb*, 53*tc*, 55*c*; **Rob Jakeway** 6–7 (background), 34–35 (background), 36–37 (background); **Dave Kesarisingh** 7*tr*, *cr* & *b*, 19*cr*; **John Lawrence** (Virgil Pomfret) 52*cl*;

Kevin Maddison 76–77; **Malcolm Porter** 20*tl* & *c*; **Luis Rey** 11; **Bernard Robinson** 53*t*; **Mike Saunders** 59*t*; **Nick Shewring** 23*tr*; **Guy Smith** 18*bl*; **Simon Tegg** 75*tl*; **Ross Watton** 74–75; **David Webb** 30–31; **Paul Wright** 18–19, 38–39.

The publishers would also like to thank the following: Hilary Bird (index), Andrew Branson, Mike Davis, Dougal Dixon, Charlotte Evans (proofreader), Jo Fletcher-Watson, Sarah Goodwin, Ian Graham, John Jamieson, Marc Wilson (digital composites 34–35, 36–37), and Terry Woodley.

The publishers would like to thank the following for supplying photographs:

Pages **6–7** Science Photo Library; **8** Planet Earth Pictures *tl*; **10** Planet Earth Pictures *tl* & *c*, Oxford Scientific Films *tr*; **12** Oxford Scientific Films *br*; **13** Oxford Scientific Films *tl*, Natural Science Photos *tr*, Planet Earth Pictures *bl*; **14** Science Photo Library *c*; **16** Frank Lane Picture Agency *tr* & *cr*, Frank Spooner Pictures *br*; **16–17** Oxford Scientific Films; **17** NRSC Ltd/Science Photo Library *cr*; **19** Science Photo Library *bl* & *r*; **20** Bryan & Cherry Alexander/NHPA *b*; **21** Natural Science Photos *tl*, Rex Features *c*, Planet Earth Pictures *b*; **22** Sandra Crossman *cl*; **24** Oxford Scientific Films *l*; **25** Images Colour Library *tl* & *c*, NHPA *b*; **26–27** The Image Bank *b*; **27** Getty Images *br*; **28** Science Photo Library *tr* & *bc*, Oxford Scientific Films *cl* & *cr*, FLPA *cr*; **29** Science Photo Library *t*; **30** BBC Natural History Unit *tl*, Oxford Scientific Films *cl*, Natural Science Photos *cr*; **31** Fred Bavendam *tl*, Planet Earth Pictures *c*, NHPA *bl*; **32** Natural Science Photos *t* & *bl*, Planet Earth Pictures *cr*, BBC Natural History Unit *bl*; **33** Ardea *t*, Planet Earth Pictures *cl*, The Image Bank *cr*, Bruce Coleman *br*; **34–35** (composite picture) Oxford Scientific Films/NHPA/Linda Dunk/FLPA/Planet Earth Pictures/Bruce Coleman/Robert Harding Associates/Rex Features; **36** Planet Earth Pictures *cl*, Oxford Scientific Films *tr*; **37** NHPA *tl* & *tc*, Oxford Scientific Films *br* & *bl*, Planet Earth Pictures *cr* & *cb*; **38** Planet Earth Pictures *cr*, NHPA *bl*; **39** Frank Spooner Pictures *t*, Planet Earth Pictures *c*, Ifremer/France *b*; **40** FLPA *tl*, Bruce Coleman *c*, Natural Science Photos *b*; **41** NHPA *tl* & *cl*, Lars-Erik Lofgren *tr*, Oxford Scientific Films *c*, Planet Earth Pictures *cr*; **42** Bruce Coleman *tl*, Oxford Scientific Films *tc* & *br*, Planet Earth Pictures *bl*; **42–43** NHPA *c*; **43** Planet Earth Pictures *tr* & *bl*, Oxford Scientific Films *br*; **44–45** Planet Earth Pictures *c*, **44** Trip *bl*, Planet Earth Pictures *br* & *tl*; **45** Planet Earth Pictures *t* & *bl*, FLPA *cr*, Oxford Scientific Films *br*; **46** Oxford Scientific Films *cl*, *bl* & *br*; **46–47** Planet Earth Pictures *c*; **47** Bruce Coleman *c*, Oxford Scientific Films *cb*, Planet Earth Pictures *br*; **48** Planet Earth Pictures *t*, Oxford Scientific Films *cr*, Natural Science Photos *bl*, NHPA *br*; **48–49** Planet Earth Pictures; **49** Planet Earth Pictures *tl* & *tr*, Oxford Scientific Films *c*, Natural Science Photos *br*; **50** Oxford Scientific Films *bl*, Natural Science Photos *cr*; **51** National Museums of Scotland/The Raymond Fortt Studios *br*; **52** Tim Severin *t*; **53** Rex Features *cr* & *b*; **54** Corbis *l*; **54–55** Mary Evans Picture Library *c*; **55** Mary Evans Picture Library *tl*, Natural Science Photos *br*; **56** Michael Holford *t*, Mary Evans Picture Library *bl*, Bridgeman Art Library *br*; **57** Bridgeman Art Library *tl* & *br*, Michael Holford *tr*, British Museum/Museum of Mankind *c*, Kos Picture Source *bl*; **58** Deep Ocean Exploration & Research *t*, AKG *b*; **59** Frank Spooner Pictures *tl*, Harbor Branch Oceanographic Institute/Florida *cl*, Planet Earth Pictures *bl*, Rex Features *br*; **60** Oxford Scientific Films *t*, Planet Earth Pictures *b*; **61** Sygma *tl* & *tr*, Rex Features *c*, Planet Earth Pictures *bl* & *br*; **62** Getty Images *bl* & *br*; **62–63** Marconi; **63** Institute of Oceanographic Services/UK *tr*, Harbor Branch Oceanographic Institute/Florida *cr*, JOIDES/Woods Hole Oceanographic Institution/USA *bl*; **64** Naval Historical Foundation *tl*, Ecoscene *bl*; **64–65** ESA *c*; **65** Institute of Oceanographic Services/UK *tr*, ESA *br*; **67** Robert Harding Associates *tl*; **69** Bruce Coleman *cl*, Getty Images *cr*; **70** detail from *Birth of Venus* (Botticelli) E. T. Archives *tl*, *The Wave* (Hokusai) Victoria & Albert Museum/Michael Holford *bl*, Ronald Grant Archives *cr*; **70–71** *The Gulf Stream* (Winslow Homer) courtesy of The Metropolitan Museum of Art; **71** Bruce Coleman *cr*, *The Beach in Front of the Casino Café* (Martha Walter) Superstock *bl*, *Birth of Venus* (Botticelli) E. T. Archives *br*; **72** Frank Spooner *c* & *b*, Rex Features *bl*; **73** Popperfoto *tl*, Robert Harding *bc*, Tony Stone *cr*, Frank Spooner *bl*; **74** Rex Features *t*, Planet Earth Pictures *b*; **75** E. T. Archives *bl* & *r*; **76** Frank Spooner Pictures *t*, Planet Earth Pictures *b*; **77** Oxford Scientific Films *tl*, Still Pictures *tr*; **78** Robert Harding Associates *b*, Oxford Scientific Films *cl*, Frank Spooner Pictures *tr*; **79** Still Pictures *tr*, Getty Images *bl*; **80–81** AFP/Press Association; **80** Planet Earth Pictures *b*; **81** Rex Features *tr*, The Mansell Collection *bl*, Oxford Scientific Films *br*; **82** NHPA *tl*, Frank Spooner Pictures *bl*, Getty Images *br*; **82–83** Rex Features; **83** NHPA *bl*, Sygma *br*; **84** Oxford Scientific Films *t*, Frank Spooner Pictures *bl* & *br*; **84–85** Planet Earth Pictures; **85** Oxford Scientific Films *cr*, Rex Features *tl*, Planet Earth Pictures *bl*; **86** Oxford Scientific Films *t*, Information & Documentation Centre for the Geography of the Netherlands/Aerocamera/Hofmeester *b*; **87** Oxford Scientific Films *t*, US Geological Survey/Army Corps of Engineers/Florida *cl*, Robert Harding Associates *cr*, Popperfoto *b*; **88** Planet Earth Pictures *tl*, *tr* & *br*; **89** Tony Stone Images.